Chicken Soup for the Soul

Devotional Stories for Wives

CALGARY PUBLIC LIBRARY

SEP - 2013

Chicken Soup for the Soul: Devotional Stories for Wives
101 Daily Devotions to Comfort, Encourage, and Inspire You
Susan M. Heim, Karen C. Talcott

Published by Chicken Soup for the Soul Publishing, LLC www.chickensoup.com
Copyright © 2013 by Chicken Soup for the Soul Publishing, LLC. All Rights Reserved.

No part of this publication may be reproduced, stored in a retrieval system or transmitted in any form or by any means, electronic, mechanical, photocopying, recording or otherwise, without the written permission of the publisher.

CSS, Chicken Soup for the Soul, and its Logo and Marks are trademarks of Chicken Soup for the Soul Publishing LLC.

The publisher gratefully acknowledges the many publishers and individuals who granted Chicken Soup for the Soul permission to reprint the cited material.

THE HOLY BIBLE, NEW INTERNATIONAL VERSION®, NIV® Copyright © 1973, 1978, 1984, 2011 by Biblica, Inc.™ Used by permission. All rights reserved worldwide.

Front cover photo courtesy of Getty Images/Digital Vision. Back cover and interior photos courtesy of iStockPhoto.com/ dra_schwartz (© dra_schwartz.)

Cover and Interior Design & Layout by Brian Taylor, Pneuma Books, LLC

Distributed to the booktrade by Simon & Schuster. SAN: 200-2442

Publisher's Cataloging-in-Publication Data
(Prepared by The Donohue Group)

Chicken soup for the soul : devotional stories for wives : 101 daily
  devotions to comfort, encourage, and inspire you / [compiled by] Susan
  M. Heim [and] Karen C. Talcott.

    p. : ill. ; cm.

  ISBN: 978-1-61159-910-7

  1. Wives--Religious life--Literary collections. 2. Christian life--Literary collections.
  3. Wives--Religious life--Anecdotes. 4. Christian life--Anecdotes. 5. Wives--Prayers
  and devotions. 6. Devotional literature. I. Heim, Susan M. II. Talcott, Karen C. III.
  Title: Devotional stories for wives : 101 daily devotions to comfort, encourage, and
  inspire you

  PN6071.W69 C45 2013
  810.8/02/092/08655   2013937411

PRINTED IN THE UNITED STATES OF AMERICA
on acid∞free paper
22 21 20 19 18 17 16 15 14 13   01 02 03 04 05 06 07 08 09 10

Chicken Soup for the Soul

for the Soul®

Devotional Stories for Wives

101 Daily Devotions to Comfort, Encourage, and Inspire You

Susan M. Heim
Karen C. Talcott

CSS

Chicken Soup for the Soul Publishing, LLC
Cos Cob, CT

www.chickensoup.com

Contents

❸

~Learning to Communicate~

❹

~Embracing Our Differences~

⑤
~Recapturing the Magic~

⑥
~Facing Our Challenges Together~

⑦
~Surrender It All~

❽
~Second Chances~

❾
~A Change in Perspective~

⑩

~Together in Strength~

Introduction

But Ruth replied, "Don't urge me to leave you or to turn back from you.
Where you go I will go, and where you stay I will stay. Your people will be my
people and your God my God..."
~Ruth 1:16

In the verse above, Ruth is expressing her commitment to stay with her mother-in-law, Naomi, through good times and bad—the very same vow we make when we get married. When we say these words, often witnessed by our family and closest friends, we are pledging to share everything with each other—our bodies, our minds and, yes, even our bank accounts. That's a huge commitment, and one not to be made lightly, because it's difficult to keep!

No marriage is perfect because no two people are perfect. But it helps to understand that God often brings people together to expand their capacity to love, to change their perspective, and to challenge them. Marriage is a journey, not a destination. By sharing our joys, working through our differences, and muddling through tough times, we often come through not only with a better marriage, but as more perfect versions of ourselves.

Thankfully, we don't have to "do" this marriage thing alone. We have a third partner—God—if we ask for His help. And as the stories in this book show, through the grace of our loving Father, wives and husbands can better meet their challenges together and communicate more clearly. They may even learn to embrace (and perhaps love) their differences! And, if they're fortunate, they may recapture the magic of new love or find a deeper, more satisfying love.

There are several ways in which you can read *Chicken Soup for the Soul: Devotional Stories for Wives*:

- **Start at the beginning!** Spend a little time with God each day by starting at the beginning of the book and reading a story each day for inspiration.

- **Pray for guidance.** Holding the book closed, pray for God to guide you to just the right devotional that you need to read that day. Randomly open the book and see where the Spirit leads!

- **Select a topic.** If you're dealing with a particular problem, scroll through the table of contents and turn to the appropriate chapter. Select a devotional that applies to your situation.

Whether you're a new bride, have been married for several years or are a veteran of this marriage business, *Chicken Soup for the Soul: Devotional Stories for Wives* will inspire you to look at your marriage — and your husband — with new eyes. As we were reading these stories, we both found a renewed appreciation for the gift of our husbands, as well as a hunger to make our relationships with them a higher priority in our busy lives. We hope it will have the same impact on you. And we pray that reading these stories will deepen your relationship with God as He guides you toward a renewed commitment to your partner and your faith.

~Susan and Karen

Chapter 1

Devotional Stories for Wives

Honoring Our Commitment

That is why a man leaves his father and mother and is united to his wife, and they become one flesh.

~Genesis 2:24

Midnight Plane to Georgia

By Jeneil Palmer Russell

With great power the apostles continued to testify to the resurrection of the Lord Jesus. And God's grace was so powerfully at work in them all…
~Acts 4:33

On Friday morning, I began receiving scripted phone calls that my husband's unit would be arriving at Fort Stewart, Georgia, after a yearlong deployment. There would be a homecoming ceremony late that night. Weeks earlier, we had decided that the girls and I would not attend. We could not be exactly sure when he'd arrive—and it was too expensive to fly to Georgia on short notice.

But as the calls came in, I suddenly knew I had to be there. It meant booking a last-minute flight, making hasty arrangements, and asking for help. I called on my sister and friends, and they gladly blessed me by caring for the girls. It was a big deal for me to spontaneously leave my children for a whole weekend. But it was important and necessary for me to put us first.

When I arrived, hundreds of people were gathered on the field: mothers, fathers, spouses, children. There was such a sense of excitement and anticipation—understandably so—as these families had been waiting over a year for their loved one to come home. Kids ran back and forth across the field. Babies were bounced and bundled. There were signs, red-white-and-blue balloons, flowers and miniature flags everywhere.

We waited and waited. I prayed for the families of soldiers who'd been lost. I thanked God for keeping this husband and father safe and bringing him home. It felt surreal to finally make it to this point, the deployment's end. I thanked God for all of the people who had loved us, supported us and prayed for us throughout the year.

At 2:30 A.M., white buses with soldiers leaning out the windows came into view. People lined the streets, cheering, waving signs and flags. It was breathtaking, and I was honored to be among the number cheering for them.

Someone sang the National Anthem. Men and women in uniform on the field and in the bleachers stood at attention. An older man standing next to me, in his Harley Davidson leather jacket, doffed his hat and belted out the words with tears streaming down his cheeks. The chaplain prayed. The general gave a speech. The Army song was sung. Finally, family and friends were ordered to "attack the formation," and people raced onto the field.

A friend of Brandon's who had once served with him in Iraq motioned for me to follow him — we had not seen Brandon yet among the 354 soldiers. I spotted him first. His head was down slightly as he walked quickly off the field. I saw a mixture of emotions on his face — relief, exhaustion, happiness, a little sadness that his family was not there. His friend embraced him. Then he said, "Hey, I've got someone here to see you..."

The look on his face when he saw me... well, then I knew it had all been worth it. All of it.

The signs at homecoming ceremonies are always colorful, personal and wonderfully decorated. But my sign was simple, and it took me just two minutes to make. I carried it with me on the plane all the way from Massachusetts, and when I saw "my soldier," I stepped back and held up my sign: WE MADE IT.

By God's grace alone.

My Prayer

Lord, thank you for chances to surprise my husband with love. Remind my heart to seek him out, to find him and never let go. Help us to treasure this gift of marriage.

Amen.

A Promise He Could Not Break

By Pat Stockett Johnston

Many are the plans in a person's heart, but it is the LORD's purpose that prevails.
~Proverbs 19:21

When my husband Gordon and I began to date in college, I already knew he felt God wanted him to pastor a church. I was okay with that except for one thing: I didn't want him to accept the pastorate of a church outside California because I wanted to live in the same state as my parents and five brothers and sisters. He promised me that would be no problem.

His first two church assignments were within an hour of my parents' home. I found that to be perfect! I happily taught first and second grade at neighboring schools during those first four years. Then one day, the unexpected happened.

We both were delegates to our church's missions convention, so I took that day off school and left our two-year-old daughter, Beverly, in the church nursery during the meetings.

The afternoon program opened with the three young daughters of the two missionary speakers singing a song in Haitian Creole. I admired their parents for being willing to raise those darling girls in Haiti.

Suddenly, during their song, I heard the voice of God speaking to me. "I want your children to sing in a foreign language."

Up to that time, I had had no desire to move to another country and serve as a missionary. But I quickly realized my children would not be singing in any language but English if we stayed in the States. I sat in a daze for a few moments, knowing God was waiting for my response. Then I recognized that what God wanted for my children, I also wanted for them. I whispered a soft "yes" and immediately felt peace flood over me.

During the middle of the evening meeting, I jabbed Gordon in the ribs (he insists it hurt!) and asked, "Have you ever thought about being a missionary?"

To my great surprise, he whispered, "God called me at noon! Has He called you?"

"Yes, while the missionary girls sang."

After the service, Gordon explained that God had given him a missionary call during lunch. "I told God no. I could not be a missionary because I had promised you I wouldn't leave California, and I could not break that promise! When you told me about your call, I realized I could now say yes to God!"

My respect and admiration for my husband's faithfulness to his promise grew. And my faith in God helped me release him from that promise and allowed us a thirty-four-year missionary career in the Middle East and Papua New Guinea. We can trust God when we are faithful to His purposes in our lives.

My Prayer

Our Heavenly Father, I thank you for a husband who keeps his promises and follows the path you set before him. It is my prayer that when your call comes, we all have the ability to listen and go wherever you lead.

Amen.

Serving Love

By Jennie Bradstreet

"Have you seen the one my heart loves?" Scarcely had I passed them when I found the one my heart loves. I held him and would not let him go...
~Song of Songs 3:3-4

Our lives had changed forever. My thirty-two-year-old husband, Erik, had tongue cancer. Within days of the diagnosis, he had gone through surgery to remove a portion of his tongue, had a tube placed for feeding, and began radiation and chemotherapy.

I couldn't bear to see him in so much pain. Because Erik couldn't speak, he mouthed directions to me, and I became his voice and his advocate, rarely leaving his side throughout most of his hospital stay.

The overworked nursing staff, with six to ten patients per shift, had little time for anything more than taking care of patients' essential needs. They rushed in and out of his room, making promises of bed changes, extra hospital supplies and even a bath, that under the circumstances, were unable to be fulfilled. So, as eleven days passed without Erik receiving a bath, anger rose in my heart, and I decided I would give him a sponge bath. Little did I know that this experience would be the most intimate moment he or I would ever share.

Placing a Please Do Not Disturb sign on the door, I assembled the preparations for his bath. Then I began by gently wiping his face, washing his eyes and downward to his neck, where sixty-four staples created a line from his ear, down his jaw line, and across his neck, ending directly under his chin. Gingerly, I washed around this very sore area, and silent tears ran down my cheeks. My heart was mourning the loss of his tongue and his face as I had always known it.

Maneuvering around tubes and drains and IV lines, I washed each inch of his body, thanking God for every bump, scar, mole and hair, cherishing every cell in Erik's body.

In my mind, I imagined Jesus washing the disciples' feet, lowering himself to a servant's role. I thought about how His gesture humbled the disciples.

In these moments, as I continued, I felt the deepest love for my husband I have ever known. To be his servant when he most desperately needed me humbled me completely. But then I realized how humbling it must have been for Erik to need help with his most basic needs.

My earlier anger with the nursing staff for their inattention melted into gratitude when I realized God had ordained this moment for Erik and me. Instead of feeling the embarrassment and humiliation of a stranger caring for him, Erik would feel my love as I, his helpmate, carried out the duties that honored him.

I looked up at Erik's face, blinking away my tears, and saw that he was crying, too. Without words, we were thinking the exact same thing, more connected than we had ever been. He looked into my eyes and mouthed, "I love you." After drying him off and covering him, I crawled into his hospital bed and laid my head on his chest, listening to my favorite sound: his heartbeat.

My Prayer

*Dear God, how great is the example that
Jesus showed His disciples. His love and
service to His followers paved a way for all of
us to find redemption. I pray that you would
use me in service to others, that through the
works of my hands, your light and love will
shine through.*

Amen.

4

The Ring

By Susan Farr Fahncke

And over all these virtues put on love,
which binds them all together in perfect unity.
~Colossians 3:14

It had been a blistering hot day, and my cool shower felt good. I had been working hard on the English garden we are building in the wild, weed-ridden back yard. As the water pounded my aching muscles, I leaned my hot forehead against the cool shower wall. Suddenly, it hit me.

My left ring finger was bare.

While working in the dirt, I had taken off my ring and laid it on the baby's folded-up playpen. I went back to work and forgot all about it. When darkness began to fall, I hauled my gardening tools and the playpen into the garage. In my eagerness to shower, I had forgotten my ring was on top of the playpen.

I slammed off the water, grabbed a towel and bolted out of the house, yelling, "My riiiiiing!"

After my husband made me go put on a robe, we armed ourselves with flashlights and began to search. To my horror, I discovered that, because I had been watering, each blade of grass sparkled like diamonds—exactly like those in my wedding band.

Knowing that the search was even more impossible with our

now sparkling lawn, I felt the tears threaten. As we wandered around the yard with our flashlights—my husband in shorts, black socks and dress shoes, and myself in my robe—I realized how *married* we were. I thought of my wedding band, and all that it meant. I knew we could go and buy another one, but this was the one we had exchanged our vows with. It had seen years of tears, love, laughing, fighting and finding our way to firm ground in our marriage. Nothing could ever replace that particular ring. Its bent, crooked circle fit us perfectly.

Thinking of the significance of that ring and how much I loved the man who gave it to me, I regretted how often I had taken my marriage for granted, how everyday life can fog the importance of those vows and how rarely I reflected upon them. Tears blurred my vision as I agonized over my carelessness.

My husband, ever the calm, faithful one, assured me we would find it. But we had searched so long and covered the same area so many times that I doubted his words. I couldn't match his faith. A few minutes later, right next to where the playpen had been, he reached down and, with a smile, held up my beautiful wedding ring, sparkling in the beam of the flashlight. I snatched it away, slipped it onto my finger, and threw my arms around him with a joyous, "Thank you!"

So relieved to have this wonderful, unending circle of our love back, I finally let the tears wash down my face and onto his neck.

Looking at my ring, each day I am reminded of the promise that holds our family together, makes our children feel safe, and signifies our commitment to each other, our children, and to God. Almost losing the ring taught me a priceless lesson: In a world where so much is fleeting, unstable and temporary, it embodies the most sacred, powerful bonds on earth. Marriage.

My Prayer

Dear Father, thank you for this gift of marriage. Please remind me each day to honor it, to be grateful for it, and to never take it for granted.

Amen.

"Look how it sparkles! All the years of love, laughter and tears have made it priceless!"

Reprinted by permission of
Stephanie Piro ©2013

5

Benevolence

By Diana M. Amadeo

Let the husband render unto the wife due benevolence:
and likewise also the wife unto the husband.
~1 Corinthians 7:3 (KJV)

"I am getting too old for this," I think, as my fourth grandchild wails in my arms. He has been fed, changed, cuddled, amused and napped. Now he cries inconsolably. What gives?

Then, as if in a hero's cape and tights, my husband of nearly forty years appears. He scoops up his grandchild and cuddles him. When this doesn't soothe the savage beast (I say affectionately), Grandpa takes him outside to take in the sky, woods, fresh air and all of God's glory. This does the trick. Grandbaby quiets and basks in the holiness of nature.

After all these years of being husband and wife, we have come to master the art of giving and receiving. But this art evolved slowly and with a great deal of effort. During our marriage, we were blessed with three children, worked both inside and outside the home, embraced a strong church life, and tried our best to roll with all the anxieties and stresses that family life brings. Through our failures and successes, we stayed strong and united.

But my hectic full-time nursing career and family life came to a grinding halt one evening after I collapsed and was sent to the hospital. My occasional vision problems, unsteady gait, falls and forgetfulness could no longer be ignored. Now I was temporarily blind, with hearing loss, protracted vomiting, and paralysis of my left side. After many tests and evaluations, it was revealed that multiple lesions peppered my brain and spinal cord. I have multiple sclerosis, and there is no cure. Now, after providing care all my life for my husband, children and patients, I was to receive care from them.

My husband could have chosen the easier path (as a great many spouses do when faced with a devastating illness) by packing up and leaving. Indeed, he often seems aloof or detached from the chaos around him. Throughout the joy, happiness, trauma and sorrow in our lives, he stays calm. When that sudden exacerbation happened, he cared for the children and our home and continued his career while I slowly recovered. With each relapse due to multiple sclerosis, he picks up the shattered pieces so I can struggle toward normalcy. The unpredictability of my disease — with its cognitive impairment, wheelchairs, canes and crutches — is distressing. But in my husband's calm, methodical way, we deal with these setbacks.

Working together with mutual respect, prayers, patience and a sense of oddball humor is in itself an act of kindness and charity — the definition of benevolence. The desire to do good to others, to foster goodwill and charitableness is the benevolence that Paul talks about in his letter to the Corinthians.

My husband returns from outside and carefully slips my grandson back into my arms. We smile and kiss. He makes being a wife, mother and grandmother easy.

My Prayer

*Dear God, help me to practice the art
of benevolence as a wife, friend, mother,
grandmother, daughter and sister. Help me be
your loving hands in this world.*

Amen.

Tested and Trusted

By Teresa Hoy

The LORD is my strength and my shield; my heart trusts in him, and he
helps me. My heart leaps for joy, and with my song I praise him.
~Psalm 28:7

Bill and I talked about many things before we were married, but we never discussed our virtues. However, it wasn't long after our wedding when I realized the important role that trust would play in our marriage.

Bill was a KC-135 pilot in the Air National Guard. His job took him all over the United States and the world. We spent more time apart than together.

I often wondered what he was doing and discovered it was easy to let doubts and damaging thoughts spiral through my mind.

Early in our marriage, I decided the only way to defeat negative thoughts that threatened to divide us was to put my complete confidence in God and demonstrate faithfulness to Bill.

"I trust you," I said one evening as we sat together. He was leaving the next morning. "I know God brought us together, and I believe He won't let anything come between us."

Bill squeezed my hand and said, "I believe that, too."

Long periods of separation were lonely for me. While Bill was exploring new places and meeting new people, I remained at home, caring for the same house, going to the same job, paying the same bills.

I ate most of my meals alone. There were no grand adventures for me, no exotic experiences. Since I was neither part of the single crowd nor part of the married couples, my social life was mostly non-existent. Faith kept me strong when self-pity struck. I prayed often, asking God to protect my marriage and keep my thoughts positive. Knowing that Bill trusted me also added to my determination to do what was right and avoid tempting situations.

One time, Bill called from Castle Air Force Base in California, where he was spending four weeks in training.

"I need to ask you something," he said. "I ran into a friend who's here training, too. We'd like to go to dinner tonight to catch up on old times. She's single, and it will be just the two of us."

"Do I know her?" I asked, amazed that he would call to see if I cared.

"I don't think so. She and I trained together several years ago."

"So, are you asking me if I mind if you two go to dinner?" He was a thousand miles away. I would never have known if he had gone out with his friend, yet he wanted my approval.

"I want you to be okay with it."

His honesty reinforced my trust. "I am," I said. "Enjoy your dinner."

Virtues, such as trust, are just empty words when spoken aloud. They only possess meaning and substance when personally acted out. I trusted Bill. In return, he trusted me. Because he trusted me, I wanted to be trustworthy.

A thread of loyalty has spun around us steadily for more than twenty-five years. Bill is now retired and home every day. Because we chose to trust God and each other, we walk a well-lighted path together, firmly bonded and free from doubt.

My Prayer

God, I trust in you for everything. Please help my husband and I to have that same trust in each other and to always be faithful to our marriage vows. I pray never to take your blessings for granted.

Amen.

7

What Would I Do Without You?

By Joan Oen

Rather, as servants of God we commend ourselves in every way:
in great endurance; in troubles, hardships and distresses;
in beatings, imprisonments and riots; in hard work, sleepless nights and
hunger; in purity, understanding, patience and kindness;
in the Holy Spirit and in sincere love...
~2 Corinthians 6:4-6

"That's really your color," I tease, pointing to my husband's lavender hospital gown. He smiles. The surgeon comes in and initials my husband's right shoulder as he gives an overview of the surgery.

Even though this is a routine rotator cuff surgery, anxiety tightens my chest as the surgeon speaks. I blink back tears. After we say goodbye, I rush to the nearest bathroom and let out a sob. I press toilet paper against my eyes, trying to stop the hot tears. What if something goes wrong? What would I do without him?

Almost seven hours later, I am lining up orange prescription bottles on the kitchen counter—a pill for nausea, one for itching, one for constipation, three for pain. I sigh as I try to memorize the instructions for each—take one tablet twice a day, take one to two every three hours with food, take one to two every four hours.

"Stay ahead of the pain," the nurse had advised. "Give him his pain pills during the night; wake him up if you have to."

So, I dutifully set my alarm to go off every three hours. Despite my efforts, once the block wears off, my husband is in excruciating pain. The next morning, we are both exhausted.

Since becoming a mom, my son is the main recipient of my nurturing and patience. Now my son is at my parents' house, and for the first time since his birth, all my attention is on my husband. The three-hour schedule and sleep deprivation reminds me of the nursing schedule for a newborn. With only one good arm and a head full of painkillers, my husband is like an infant, needing me to survive. It feels good to play the role of caretaker for my spouse, to have this time together, just the two of us. I am proving my love through faithful administration of pills and ice packs.

The next morning, I bring my husband a bowl of Fruit Loops along with his next dose of morphine. My heart goes out to him as I enter the bedroom. He's slumped against a mountain of pillows, right arm in a sling, looking miserable. He winces as he tries to sit up.

"Do you want me to feed you?" I ask.

He nods. I am a bit surprised that this often stubborn, incredibly independent man just agreed to let me feed him. I don't give him a chance to change his mind. I scoot close and carefully guide colorful spoonfuls into his mouth. I smile with pleasure as I feed him. I love this man in health, and now I love him in sickness. When the bowl is empty, I kiss his slightly fevered forehead and start to get up. He reaches out with his good hand and catches my arm.

"What would I do without you?" he says.

"I feel the same way, babe," I reply, my voice thick with emotion. "I love you, too."

My Prayer

*Dear Creator, grant me the patience and
wisdom to help my husband through times of
sickness. May my husband and I experience
your strength, and may love remain foremost
in our minds during the healing process.*

Amen.

Unlikely Wife

By Alma Barkman

*"Isn't there an acceptable woman among your relatives
or among all our people?..."*
~Judges 14:3

The above question posed to Samson by his parents was essentially the same question my husband's mother asked of him when we began dating. In her mind, I did not fit the model of a future daughter-in-law. I was too young to be responsible, too incapable of being a homemaker, of a different background, could not understand the dialect she spoke, and did not come from a Christian family. Surely he could find someone more suitable.

My husband ignored her negative comments, and we continued dating. When we were married four years later, she gave us her reluctant blessing, but I was very much aware that I was going to be on trial for years to come.

When our first son arrived prematurely, she wondered whether I would be a responsible mother to the little scrap of humanity I had produced. By comparison, she had given birth to nine big, bouncing babies. Our son flourished and grew despite her misgivings, as did our other three children, so eventually I passed that test.

I learned to cook and bake and sew, much to my mother-in-law's surprise. Her hunch that only Mennonite girls can cook was somewhat undermined when she discovered that some of the rest of us are actually handy in the kitchen. At one point, she indirectly conceded that my cinnamon rolls actually surpassed hers—quite the coup in her books. And she was pleased to see that I sewed most of the clothes for the entire family.

Despite my different background, she came to realize that as wives and mothers, the values that mattered—caring for our children, loving our husbands, leading a healthy lifestyle—were actually the same. Although I never did learn to speak her dialect, we communicated well in English.

As for having no religious background, that did not stand in the way of making my own personal commitment to follow Christ and becoming an active member in an evangelical church. As for my age, responsibilities have a way of maturing people beyond their years, and I was one of them.

In time, I came to realize why my mother-in-law was initially reluctant to accept me: fear. Fear of the unknown. Fear that I would disappoint her son. Fear that I would not be a competent helpmate. Fear that my values would not be solid. Fear that her grandchildren would not be given Christian training. And although her fears were legitimate, I wish she could have foreseen what Samson's parents discovered in retrospect—that they "did not know that this was from the LORD…" (Judges 14:4). Through God's unfathomable grace, we have been happily married for fifty-six years.

My Prayer

Lord, help me to recognize that some fears are understandable. Encourage me not to let them stand in the way of fulfilling your purpose in my life. Thank you for being the example that we can look to for help.

Amen.

Amazed by Grace

By Phyllis Tomberg Giglio

And now these three remain: faith, hope and love.
But the greatest of these is love.
~1 Corinthians 13:13

"Your husband has stage four lung cancer." Those chilling words were as unfamiliar to me as if the doctor had spoken a foreign language. In the coming weeks, however, those words became etched in my mind.

I knew Sal had become very sick. He coughed all the time and had lost a lot of weight. But, as usual, he refused to see a doctor. He liked to say, "My body heals itself." And most of the time, he was right.

That morning was different. When he awoke, he said, "I have to go to the hospital." We brought him to the emergency room where he had immediate treatment to remove the fluids around his heart and lungs. These fluids showed the cancer. When he came home from the hospital four weeks later, he was extremely weak and frail, so unlike the former "Macho Man" image he worked hard to maintain. He needed my help in everything—walking, dressing, getting out of bed, etc.

Sal and I had a wonderful family. Sal was a great provider, and I was immersed in taking care of our growing family over the years.

Outwardly, it appeared as though we were a big, happy family, but that was not always true. The middle years of our marriage were chaotic, with many accusations and arguments. Sal had acquired new friends, and it seemed as though he no longer loved me. I felt abandoned. In spite of his excessive drinking and lifestyle, Sal was very healthy. Yet a voice in my head was telling me I should leave him or I could wind up with a sick old man to take care of. Now the very scenario I had feared was happening.

What I didn't count on was God's grace, his unmerited favor. Somehow, God placed an overwhelming love in my heart for my husband. It was a love so powerful that I wanted only to be near him and care for him.

One morning, he awoke and was having difficulty breathing. I told his hospice nurse I needed to get into bed and hold him. She understood. It was such a precious time as I lay next to him. I told him I loved him and completely forgave him. For the first time, we prayed together, something I had hoped for since I became a Christian thirty years ago. Sal died peacefully that evening surrounded by all his children.

The memories of our last weeks together have swallowed up the painful years of our marriage. I find solace in knowing I was able to truly forgive Sal, but it wasn't something I could have accomplished on my own. God's grace is truly amazing!

My Prayer

Dear God, help us to extend forgiveness to each other. Show us how to truly love, not just with words, but by our actions. Guide us and direct us so that others will see Christ in our lives.

Amen.

10

That Was Love

By Diane Gardner

...serve one another humbly in love.
~Galatians 5:13

It was the basket. Not the Colombian roses or the diamond necklace or the theater tickets John bought me back when he sought me as his wife. No, a cheap plastic basket of laundry taught me what real love is. It was shortly after we wed, when I was dying.

Four months after we married, I entered the hospital. My body had simply stopped absorbing any food or nutrition. Not one ounce. I was literally wasting away. For weeks, my new husband stayed with me in the hospital as doctors searched for the cause and performed two surgeries to remove the portion of my system that Crohn's disease had destroyed.

But something my husband did during my recovery spoke to me of real love more than anything else. He did the laundry. Oh, not just normal laundry. When recovering from this kind of surgery, well, let's just say one's body doesn't always get timely signals for certain things. And some of the laundry was, frankly, unpleasant. I was well enough to handle the worst of it, and new bride enough to be embarrassed to ask my husband to. One evening, I woke up from resting, desperate to drop in a small load of no-longer-sexy underwear, when my husband walked into the room with the laundry—freshly washed and folded. I looked at him with tears in my eyes.

And I realized... that was love. Real, lasting love. Love that proves, through action, that it's willing to get down in the ugliest, most embarrassing parts of life with you. Love that accepts your most humiliating moments and carries you through them.

Through the tears, my eyes opened. I realized that sometimes love isn't expressed by flowers and jewelry, or even "I love you." The most powerful love is revealed through humble sacrifice. That's the love God wants us to show.

I decided I'd pay attention to the little things that spoke love, not just the big ones. You see, I saw that:

When John sent me out of state for three months so I could be with my dying father... that was love.

When he changed jobs so we could move closer to my mom... that was love.

When he took on a second job so I could pursue my dream of writing and editing... that was love.

When he fixes the computer I always break; when he insists our eggs be fixed the way I want more often than the way he prefers; when he calls me every day before he drives home... that all is love.

And it makes all the difference to recognize how my husband expresses love, rather than only noticing the flowers and candy. I've found a deeper, stronger romance. And God calls me to love sacrificially, as well. You see, I discovered that getting down in the dirty laundry together... well, that is love—love that makes marriages last.

My Prayer

Heavenly Father, please help me to recognize the little things my husband does that show love, not just the traditionally "romantic" things. And show me ways, large and small, that I can serve my husband with sacrificial love each day.

Amen.

11

Chicken Soup for the Soul

The Season Called Marriage

By Dayna E. Mazzuca

There is a time for everything, and a season for every activity under the heavens...
~Ecclesiastes 3:1

This past Christmas, my husband and I celebrated our tenth anniversary. We cozied up in front of the fire and looked back over our shared seasons.

Practically speaking, we've experienced four major moves, raising two children, job changes and several deaths in the family.

We've also experienced something less tangible. Each year, we've grown closer, sharing thoughts, dreams and desires. I believe God honors a commitment to the long haul. There have been seasons of pulling together, and seasons of pulling apart. Without the long view, we'd be in sad shape. Yet, He has made us stronger and better for having each other.

How did we do it? How does anyone do it? After twenty years of living with roommates, I thought I was ready for marriage. In reality, it was a huge adjustment. Huge.

Being married is different from having a roommate. It doesn't take friendly feelings to be married; it takes grit. It takes swallowing my pride, carrying my cross and sometimes biting my tongue. Other times, it means speaking up and learning to ask for what I need, or sitting still long enough to hear my husband's side of a story.

Ecclesiastes, chapter 3, says there is a season for everything. This includes "a time to be silent and a time to speak" (Ecclesiastes 3:7b). This chapter on the give-and-take nature of life has meant a lot to me in my marriage. As a roommate, if I had something to say, I'd call a house meeting or leave a note on the kitchen counter. If things went south, the worst I could expect was finding new digs. As a wife, the stakes are higher. My patience is lower. And a "good time to talk" is often non-existent.

For the sake of the long haul, there is indeed a time to be silent and a time to speak. A time to keep (a nasty criticism to myself) and a time to throw away (an old grudge or insecurity perhaps). A time to weep (sometimes alone, but more likely with my spouse), and a time to laugh (even when bills are piled sky high!). A time to embrace (I love when he pulls me into his arms in our nook of a kitchen), and a time to refrain from embracing (and give each other space to figure something out). There are seasons.

Our marriage is a decade-long calendar of different seasons. We've seen ten years together as husband and wife, but it feels like we've lived through a lifetime of these seasonal ups and downs, hopes and prayers. We give. We take. And somehow it all works out, according to God's design.

My Prayer

Lord, thank you for this season of life called marriage. Thank you for someone who is willing to walk with me, learn with me and just be with me. Give us both winter-time patience, summer-time joy, spring-like hope, and fall-like appreciation for your deep and lasting commitment to us.

Amen.

Chapter

2

*Devotional
Stories for
Wives*

The Power of Prayer

*I call on you, my God, for you will answer me;
turn your ear to me and hear my prayer.*

~Psalm 17:6

Just Muddle Through

By Barbara Brady

It is God who arms me with strength and keeps my way secure.
~2 Samuel 22:33

When my husband began a new job and we moved to a different city, our family's life changed drastically. Uneasy about his new job, my husband worked long hours. When he was home, he became withdrawn and depressed. Our kids grumbled about leaving their friends and rebelled about attending a new school. To add to the problems, our teenage daughter developed a physical problem requiring hospitalization and surgery in a city sixty miles away. I found myself torn between caring for our daughter, trying to find ways to help our boys adjust, and coping with my husband's discontent.

While our daughter recovered in the hospital, I stayed nearby with an elderly friend who possessed a strong Christian faith. I respected her wisdom and hoped she might have a solution for my turmoil. Ready to crack with frustration, worried sick about my family, and feeling like a total failure as a wife and mother, I blubbered to Carolyn, "What should I do? How can I help my family survive this mess?"

Carolyn did not hesitate to answer, but her advice shocked me.

"Well," she said, "pray a lot and just muddle through." Could the answer to my worries be that simple?

As I contemplated her answer, a new realization hit me. In my arrogance, I had thought I could solve everyone's problems. As a caring wife and mother, I felt I should know all the answers and somehow magically make everything okay. I wrestled with guilt because I had not been able to create happiness and contentment for everyone. Carolyn's answer helped me recognize I was not a perfect person capable of making life smooth for all my loved ones. Sometimes that is not possible.

I did what my friend suggested. I turned my struggles over to God in prayer, and I muddled through. As a family, we eventually survived the adjustments that came with the move, and in time our daughter got well. Our family still experienced some rough times, but we managed.

Now I know it is not my responsibility to fix all the problems and make everyone happy all the time. I will always try my best to be a good wife and mother, but many days all I can do is pray a lot and just muddle through. God understands our limitations.

My Prayer

*Dear Lord, I find myself struggling with the
need for perfection in my life. Help me to
turn my struggles over to you in prayer. With
your guidance, I can become the wife, mother,
and woman you created me to be.*

Amen.

13

Labor of Love

By Katie Cromwell Johnson

"...If you believe, you will receive whatever you ask for in prayer."
~Matthew 21:22

woke up on the morning of Labor Day, 1999, feeling a bit groggy and uncomfortable. It was nice to have a day off from school. While I loved my new job teaching at my alma mater, being nine months pregnant had taken its toll. I rolled over to get more comfortable, and my water broke. I called my husband, and we were off on the newest and most exciting adventure of our lives.

After arriving at the hospital, our adventure turned from exciting to worrisome. My pain was intense as my aunt allowed me to squeeze her hand tightly, talking to me in low, soft tones to get me through. My husband kept a steady watch on the baby's heart monitor, the nurses coming and going, and the look on the doctor's face. With every contraction, our son's heart rate would drop drastically low. The concerned look on my husband's face mirrored that of the doctor's. But the doctor continued to just monitor what was happening with me, as well as the five or six other women who had also gone into labor, ironically, on Labor Day.

Finally, we heard one of the nurses ask the doctor, "Are you going to call the anesthesiologist, or am I?" We were headed for a C-section. After the doctor told us, I was relieved, but one look at my husband's face told me that he wasn't. My husband, who had pulled many a calf from a struggling mama cow, was more worried than before about his wife and child. When everyone left us alone for a few minutes, tears started to well up in his eyes. He held my hands tightly and looked at me with such love. In all our time together, I had never seen my husband, such a tough cowboy, cry.

"Honey, are you okay?" He simply shook his head. That was when I knew it was time to call on God. We had prayed off and on as a couple, but it was not a regular thing.

"Do you want to pray?" He nodded.

I prayed a simple prayer that God would protect us both and bring our son safely into this world. I also prayed for peace and contentment for my husband. After praying, we shared a few more tears, a hug and a kiss. Then I was wheeled off to the delivery room.

Our son, after struggling with the cord wrapped twice around his neck, was delivered safely, and our fears turned to joy and a sense of relief. God had seen him and us through.

Since then, God has blessed us with another son. Now, not a night goes by that we don't pray together as a family, taking turns. And when it's my husband's turn, he never fails to say a prayer of gratitude for our children.

My Prayer

Lord, remind me today of the things that truly matter and help me to let go of my fears. I know that you are with me and will always bring peace and contentment when I pray in faith, believing.

Amen.

14

A Steeper Mountain to Climb

By Sarah E. Wessels

*Now faith is confidence in what we hope for
and assurance about what we do not see.*
~Hebrews 11:1

I sat in church alone again, the seat beside me cold. Couples came in, two by two. Husbands draped an arm across their wife's shoulders. Wives squeezed their husband's hands as they sang along together. Every ounce of me longed for my husband to be there beside me. My walk with the Lord was new and fresh, yet I felt the tug of guilt as I wondered, "Had I left my husband behind?" It seemed as though I had climbed a mountain and left him on the other side. I couldn't see the day when he would join me.

I have loved my husband since I was fifteen years old, so sitting alone was foreign, lonely. Knowing he wasn't ready, and fearing I might push him in the opposite direction if I pressured him, created a cloud over my newfound joy. I was convinced that the changes he witnessed in me would move his heart. I needed to have faith. God loved him more than I ever could and would get him there, but waiting was agony.

Just when I thought it would never happen, one ordinary spring day I stumbled into the kitchen, both arms weighted with groceries. On the counter, I found a note on college-ruled paper, creased in the middle. A lopsided heart drawn in pencil encircled my name, printed in familiar script. The words inside were smudged where his hand had moved along the page. The first words—sentiments of love and happiness—made me smile.

But the lines that followed put me on my knees. "You have brought me closer to God, which has been hard for me. But because of you, I know that God loves me, and He has a plan for me. And a big part of that plan was you." Simple words, but a complete fulfillment of prayer.

Lonely church days are a memory now. I have come to realize that I didn't leave behind my husband; he just had a steeper mountain to climb. Even when I could not see it, God was working through me. Faith, patience and prayer provided a hand for me to hold on Sundays.

My Prayer

*Father God, thank you for your promises.
Thank you for giving me faith that you could
move a man up a mountain. Thank you for
guiding his path. And mostly, Lord, thank you
that our paths now head toward you, together,
hand in hand.*

Amen.

15

God's financial Plan

By Jeanette Hurt

"Come to me, all you who are weary and burdened, and I will give you rest…"
~Matthew 11:28

It was one of those "Dear Lord, what are we going to do?" moments. My husband Kyle called me from work to tell me he had just lost half his salary. Under normal circumstances, it would have been difficult, but I would have simply taken on more of our bills.

But at the time Kyle's architecture firm announced these drastic cuts, I was eight months pregnant and on bed rest, and I had already had to severely curtail my freelance writing business. Kyle and I had also been planning to have me become the primary caregiver of our son once he was born. This announcement sent us into a tailspin.

Later that night, when Kyle got home, we sat down with a stack of our monthly bills. But before we even began looking through them, we reached across the table to hold hands and pray. I don't remember exactly what we said, but I know that we praised God for His infinite goodness, for the plans He had for us, and for the plans He had for our little son, still inside my womb. We affirmed that though the news looked awful, we were not the one who was all-powerful, all-seeing, and eternal. Our perspective was limited, whereas God's is limitless.

Then we took out a pad and a pencil, breaking down our monthly expenses to the penny, and we started slashing. No more lunches out. No more gourmet groceries. No more movie rentals. Instead, Kyle packed a lunch for work, we began shopping at a discount grocery store, and we checked out movies from the library.

We had always lived frugally, but now we had our expenses pared down to the absolute essentials. We took a deep breath, swallowed our pride and investigated public assistance. Unfortunately, we learned we made sixteen dollars too much per week to qualify.

We had no wiggle room, and we were scared. There were many nights when our fears and worries woke us up and prevented us from restful sleep.

That's when we stormed heaven. There's nothing quite like the power that comes from praising the Lord in the middle of your troubles. And anytime it seemed like our situation would stay bleak, we received unexpected assistance. A new—and easy—client hired me to write a monthly column. Our acupuncturist agreed to trade services. Our midwife cut her fees in half. These blessings helped us stay on track, and we thanked and praised God for each one of them.

It wasn't easy, and as we lived through it, it seemed like it would never end. But then, suddenly, seven months after our son was born, a new architecture firm contacted Kyle out of the blue. He was hired on the spot, and his new job more than replaced his lost salary and benefits.

Through this challenge, our marriage grew stronger, our faith increased, and we discovered our true priorities: God, then marriage and family. As long as we had our priorities straight, God would help us pay the bills.

My Prayer

*Lord, we bring our current financial troubles
to the foot of your cross, where you bore our
burdens. Please, through the blessed help
of your Holy Spirit, guide us with wisdom,
discernment and understanding to see what
your priorities are for our lives and our
marriage.*

Amen.

16

The Powerful Gift of Prayer

By Diane Stark

The prayer of a righteous person is powerful and effective.
~James 5:16b

We'd been home from our honeymoon just a few weeks when I found the book. It was called *The Power of a Praying Husband*, by Stormie Omartian. I flipped through it and realized it instructed husbands on how to better pray for their wives. The fact that my new husband had purchased such a book was quite a shocker—in a really good way.

I noted that the bookmark was nestled in at page 17. A few days later, I checked again. The bookmark had moved to page 33. The next time I looked, it had moved to page 56. My husband not only owned a book about how to pray for me, but he was actually reading it. It was then that I knew I had truly hit the jackpot in the husband department.

Wanting to be as good a spouse as Eric was to me, I began to pray for him, too. But my heart wasn't really in it. Eric was praying deep prayers for my spiritual wellbeing, while my prayers usually went something like this: "Dear God, bless Eric and help him to have a good day today. Amen."

Eric was clearly the "better half" in our relationship.

I discovered there was a companion book called *The Power of a Praying Wife*. I ran to the Christian bookstore and bought their last copy.

Although I enjoyed the book, I still struggled with praying for Eric. My prayers were awkward and unfocused, but I felt obligated to pray for him because I knew he was praying for me. I asked God to give me an earnest desire to pray for my husband, and God answered that prayer in a surprising way.

While reading the book one day, I noticed something odd. The inside cover had writing on it. It was an inscription that read, "Dear Kelly, On your wedding day, we wanted to tell you how happy we are that you are marrying our son. We prayed for many years that he would find someone like you. Now we ask that you pray for our son, as a gift to him. Welcome to the family. Love, Jim and Susan."

I smiled. It seemed clear that Kelly had received the book as a wedding present from her new in-laws. She either already owned the book or was already such a prayer warrior that she didn't need the advice. She returned the book to the store, and I bought it.

Although the words Kelly's in-laws wrote weren't meant for me, I've learned from them. I now pray for my own children's future spouses. And praying for Eric no longer feels like an obligation. I remember that praying for him is a gift I can give him—a powerful, life-changing gift.

Faithfully praying for my husband has become more than a task on a to-do list. It's become yet another way to love him.

My Prayer

Dear Lord, thank you that you hear our prayers and care about our concerns. Help us to develop a habit of praying for our husbands. May we always remember that praying for someone is the most important gift we can give them.

Amen.

The Perfect Coffee Table

By Tina Friesen

Do you not know? Have you not heard? The LORD is the everlasting God,
the Creator of the ends of the earth. He will not grow tired or weary,
and his understanding no one can fathom. He gives strength to the weary
and increases the power of the weak.
~Isaiah 40:28-29

My husband and I don't always see eye to eye. We're not alone in this, I've discovered. Our marriage is evidence that opposites do attract. For instance, I like pop music and soft rock, and I play the piano. My husband plays the banjo and loves bluegrass. I like to plan and host parties while he prefers an intimate family dinner. He likes a firm bed, while I like a bit of softness, at least enough so that my shoulders don't hurt when I sleep on my side. I could go on.

So, when we decided to go shopping for a coffee table, after about forty minutes of looking around the furniture store, my stomach began to hurt and my head began to pound. We were not agreeing on anything. I had narrowed down my choices to two tables. He had done the same. I looked at his tables and knew I couldn't live with them. He felt precisely the same way about mine.

At this point, I was near tears, and I wandered off by myself for a bit to have a little talk with God. I said, "God, you put the two of us together, and you know how different we are. This comes as no surprise to you. I have to believe, however, that there is a coffee table out there that we can agree on. I believe this because all things are possible with you."

After my prayer, I walked a little farther and saw another table I liked. I was surprised I hadn't seen it before. And I thought that my husband might actually like this one, too. So I called him over to look at it. By this time, he was ready to go home. He had done enough looking for one night. But it turned out to be the one table in the entire store that we could agree on. I was so delighted I almost shed tears of joy. God confirmed to me in that moment that He can and will make a way for us.

Later, I discovered that my brother and his wife bought the same coffee table! When I summarized our story, they told me their experience was very similar to ours. Our coffee tables now symbolize God's faithfulness.

My Prayer

Heavenly Father, I thank you for your infinite wisdom. You encourage us to seek you and discover the design you have for our lives. Although we, as couples, may not always see eye to eye, we ask you to help us to find common ground in our marriage and grow together in love.

Amen.

"We call this our 'miracle' coffee table. It's a miracle we found one we agreed on!"

Reprinted by permission of
Stephanie Piro ©2013

18

Answered Prayers

By Nancy Peacock

"Because he loves me," says the LORD, "I will rescue him; I will protect him, for he acknowledges my name. He will call on me, and I will answer him; I will be with him in trouble, I will deliver him and honor him. With long life I will satisfy him and show him my salvation."
~Psalm 91:14-16

Tomorrow was Thanksgiving Day. Today was chaotic as last-minute preparations for a family reunion consumed the whole local family. My husband had indigestion—or so he thought. I worked around him as he helped set up tables and chairs, vacuum the breakfast room and take things to the freezer. In the early afternoon, he complained of his arm hurting. I hustled him in the car—never thinking to call an ambulance—and took him to our walk-in clinic to see a doctor we had known for years.

He sat on the examining table while the nurse took his temperature and blood pressure. Everything seemed normal, and she left. I stood beside him with my arms around him and made some silly joke. He laughed at me. But then his arm flew up, his glasses went flying, and he went into cardiac arrest. I clutched him so he wouldn't fall to the floor and screamed for the doctor.

Our friend called a Code Blue, helped me lay him back on

the examining table, and started cardiac resuscitation as the nurse brought in the crash cart. I backed into a corner and watched. Was my beloved husband of thirty-eight years dying?

There was only one thing I could do to help—pray. "Lord, he is yours, and he needs you now." Then I prayed the hardest words anyone can say: "Thy will be done."

Endless minutes passed as the medical team worked frantically. A cardiologist came into the room and made decisions. An ambulance waited to transport my husband to a nearby hospital if resuscitation efforts were successful. And, thank God, they were.

I went in the ambulance with him and filled out forms in Admitting while he was taken to Intensive Care. Someone asked me to wait in a little room across from the entrance to the Intensive Care Unit. I called my children and our pastor. While I paced nervously and waited, I idly opened a Bible to a random page. The words I read stunned me:

"Because he loves me," says the LORD, "I will rescue him; I will protect him, for he acknowledges my name. He will call on me, and I will answer him; I will be with him in trouble, I will deliver him and honor him. With long life I will satisfy him and show him my salvation" (Psalm 91:14-16).

The words were true. My husband not only lived, but thrived, and he is a blessing to me, his children and his grandchildren. Thank you, Lord.

My Prayer

Dear Lord, I am so thankful that you are a loving God who intimately hears my prayers. I know that you will never desert me when I am feeling scared or overwhelmed. Help me to surrender my will to yours and find peace.

Amen.

Even If

By Dawn M. Lilly

You will keep in perfect peace those whose minds are steadfast,
because they trust in you.
~Isaiah 26:3

"Have you heard?" my neighbor asked. "A plane went down. Jim called and told me he's okay, but he couldn't say anything more. Communication at both squadrons has been shut down. Have you heard from Dave?"

"No," I said, realizing for the first time that my brave and strong husband wasn't invincible. Fear paralyzed me as I hung up the phone.

Dave was an Air Force pilot and he was at the squadron flying that day. I was home caring for our toddler.

All I could do was stand there and think back on that morning. Dressed in his flight suit, Dave had walked into the kitchen and grabbed his sack lunch. Then he kissed me goodbye. "I'll see you for dinner," he said as he stepped out the door. But we really had no guarantee that his words were true.

One hour slowly slipped into two. Laundry never made it from the washer to the dryer, and dishes stacked up in the sink. Outside, a deadly hush fell over our neighborhood on the pilot training base as anxious wives stayed indoors by their phones.

When Dave called several hours later, I dropped to my knees in thanksgiving. Later that evening, I learned that a base jet had crashed during a routine solo flight. The pilot was killed. I didn't know him, but I had no doubt a mother and perhaps a sweetheart mourned for him that day. I realized I couldn't always count on my husband to be there for me.

That was more than thirty years ago. My prayer for Dave changed that day. I realized that while I could count on him to be a faithful and loving husband and father, I couldn't always be sure that he would look both ways before he crossed the street, chew thoroughly before swallowing, or land his plane safely after each and every takeoff. I couldn't even know for sure that he would fall asleep next to me in the evening and wake back up the next morning.

Dave no longer flies fighters for the Air Force, but he is no less adventurous. He flew an experimental jet while Navy ships fired live ammunition at the target he towed behind it. He suffered severe altitude sickness while hiking in the Himalayas. And he laughed when asked to sign a waiver before whitewater rafting with crocodiles in Panama.

Today, Dave is sailing on Puget Sound. Since the thought of dodging ferries and freighters through a thick blanket of fog terrifies me, I declined his invitation. But as I prayed for him this morning, I felt God ask me to let go of the "what ifs" and to trust in no one and nothing but Him. The Lord reminded me that only He can quiet my fearful spirit. Only He can give me peace.

My Prayer

Father, thank you for blessing me with this wonderful man. As I encourage him to be the adventurous person you created him to be, help me to leave him in your hands and to trust you to know what is best — even if he doesn't return home to me this evening.

Amen.

20

Get Out of the Way

By Johnna Stein

*But when you pray, go into your room, close the door and pray
to your Father, who is unseen. Then your Father, who sees what is done
in secret, will reward you.*
~Matthew 6:6

After four years of marriage, my husband and I became
Christians the very same weekend. I assumed that
meant we would follow the same smooth path of loving
the Lord and growing in our faith together at a steady
pace. We got off to a great start when Frank suggested we join a newly
formed couples group in our church. It was a wonderful experience
as we began reading the Bible together and learning how to raise our
two young kids in the faith.

However, after a few years and an overseas move, it seemed
that I was reading my Bible, doing devotions and exploring my faith
more than my husband. We still attended a couples group that we
both enjoyed, but I felt like I was somehow getting too far ahead
of my husband. So I told him and began "helping" him in his faith
journey. I shared with him how he could best choose a devotional
book, and pray more and better. I did all I could to move him along.
When attending women's conferences, I made sure I picked up a
special book or devotion that was just perfect for him. I was full of

helpful hints. For example, whenever he read the newspaper, I would jest, "Might want to read some Good News to go along with that bad news!"

But no matter how I approached the situation, nothing seemed to motivate him. All my ideas backfired. Finally, I confided in an older, wiser woman in our church, and she recommended I pray for him. Not do anything else. Just pray. What a concept! It was harder than it seemed. Although I know prayer is one of the most important aspects of a believer's life, it didn't feel like I was taking action. Perhaps that's what God had in mind—that I would stop acting and get out of the way.

At first, I saw no immediate results. It was hard to resist the temptation to express my view of my husband's spiritual life. Sometimes I failed and just had to say something, and I always regretted it. I knew I needed to pray and get out of the way. So I finally did.

Shortly thereafter, my husband was asked to be on the church vestry. This seemed to be the catalyst that drove him to regularly read his Bible and prepare well for those sometimes challenging vestry meetings. The positive trend continued as we taught two courses together for adults and teens. He dug deeper into the Word, and his faith deepened.

My husband found his way, just not my way. His style is different; his rhythm is different; his growth is different. I tend to grow in my faith in measured steps, while Frank grows in leaps and bounds. He caught up to me in no time! And sometimes he rolls right past me. All I needed to do was get out of the way and pray!

My Prayer

Heavenly Father, I praise you and thank you for my wonderful husband. I surrender him and his spiritual life into your mighty hands. Help me to recognize the times when I need to let go of the need to control the outcome and just bring my concerns to you in prayer.

Amen.

21

Emergency Room Prayer

By Amelia Rhodes

Answer me when I call to you, my righteous God.
Give me relief from my distress; have mercy on me and hear my prayer.
~Psalm 4:1

After rushing the kids to the bus stop, I found my husband immobilized by pain on our bathroom floor. He had suffered from occasional back pain, but nothing like the sudden and extreme pain of that morning. I sat next to him, tears silently streaming down my face, as we tried to figure out what to do. The only thing I could pray was, "Please, God, help him. Please help."

I finally called an ambulance, and we spent the remainder of the day in an emergency room hallway. He suffered back spasm after back spasm. My own body stiffened with each attack. The doctors pumped him full of painkillers and muscle relaxers, but nothing helped.

After six hours, and no sign of improvement, I went to the bathroom and cried in a stall.

"God, I don't even know what to ask the doctors to do. Please send help!"

Not long after my desperate bathroom-stall prayer, God sent help in the form of a neighbor's phone call.

"I saw the ambulance in your driveway this morning and wanted to check to see if you were all okay," she said.

"I'm afraid we're not okay. I'm at the hospital with my husband," I replied.

I filled her in on the details, knowing that she had suffered from serious back pain for years.

"You need to insist that he gets an MRI to find out what's going on. Keep insisting until they do one," she said.

I thanked her and immediately asked to see the attending doctor. The doctor wanted to keep the current course, but I insisted on an MRI.

The doctor warned me that it might take eight hours before there was an opening, and I prepared myself for a long night of waiting.

Not more than a half-hour later, the orderlies came to take my husband for the MRI. The doctors and nurses said they had never seen anyone get in that quickly. I smiled, knowing that God had paved the way for us as an answer to prayer.

The MRI showed two bulged disks. After an injection into the affected disks, my husband finally experienced relief. And praise God, after months of therapy, he received complete healing.

That day in the emergency room reminded me that no matter how simple the prayer—or where it is offered from—God is listening and ready to help us. We just need to humbly ask for help.

My Prayer

*Lord, please help us to remember to pray for
our husbands, no matter what the situation or
wherever we might be. May we never be too
busy to stop and ask for your help.*

Amen.

22

Mr. Fix-It

By Dena Netherton

Be joyful in hope, patient in affliction, faithful in prayer.
~Romans 12:12

When I first met my husband, Bruce, we were frugal graduate students at the University of Michigan. He had an old car that required frequent maintenance to keep it running. Sometimes our dates would look more like a high school car repair class. I'd shine a flashlight into the belly of the motor, and Bruce would explain what he was doing with all those confusing wires and hoses.

When we got married, I naturally assumed that my new husband could fix anything. After all, my dad also worked on the family car. In addition, he could knock down walls in our house, build bookcases, put in whole bathrooms, and even construct a brick staircase. I thought that's what all men could do.

It came as a shock when I discovered the truth. One day, our faithful bedside table lamp no longer worked. So I brought the thing to my husband and said, "Could you find out what's wrong with this and fix it?"

Bruce said, "Oh, just throw it out. It'll cost more to fix it than it's worth."

I never told Bruce how disappointed I was, but I sure prayed about it. Money was tight in those early days of our marriage, and when the kids started coming, it became even more important that we live frugally.

I was a young wife, with lots to learn. But two things that God taught me were to focus on my husband's wonderful qualities, not on that one disappointing "flaw," and to keep praying for him.

To my surprise, as the years passed, Bruce learned to fix broken toilets, replace bathroom tiles, repair broken bikes, and set up and take down swing sets and jungle gyms.

Of course, my husband never achieved superstar status as a fix-it man. Certainly not like my dad. But then, my dad never learned to play the drums like Bruce, or teach Bible lessons for the whole church, or direct a church choir, or successfully manage an entire quality control department for a sizable corporation.

Bruce took the kids camping and river rafting. They climbed rocks and trees, and he taught them how to roast the perfect marshmallow. Bruce listened to the children as they recited their Bible verses. He rocked them at night when they were ill. He listened, too, when their hearts were broken by the neighborhood bully or the girl next door. He offered sympathy, advice, and encouragement.

And today, when my grown sons have a question about work or marriage or childrearing, it's usually Bruce they talk to.

I'm glad the Lord helped me to pray for my husband throughout the years. I'm sure my children will agree: Bruce has become Mr. Fix-it.

My Prayer

Lord, I ask you to bless my marriage. Help me to see the best in my husband and to persevere in prayer for him.

Amen.

Chapter 3

Devotional Stories for Wives

Learning to Communicate

*Always be prepared to give an answer to everyone who asks you
to give the reason for the hope that you have.
But do this with gentleness and respect...*

~1 Peter 3:15

23

What'd I Say?

By Debra Ayers Brown

We are from God, and whoever knows God listens to us...
~1 John 4:6

Balancing a bag of groceries in one arm, I pushed the kitchen door open. My daughter Meredith, home from college, followed me, talking a mile a minute.

"Mom," she said as I set down everything, "you're not listening."

"I am listening."

"Then what'd I say?"

I repeated it verbatim. So Meredith continued talking to the back of my head as I put away the groceries and started the spaghetti. Water boiled. Spicy sauce simmered. All the while, I tried to follow Meredith's monologue.

"Uh-huh," I mumbled.

Soon, my husband Allen's keys clanked into his tray by the door. He gave me the rundown on his day.

"Um," I said and prepared the salad.

He went on and on about the upcoming South Carolina game, about injuries, players, Gamecock Central posts, and which buddies were going to the game.

"Really?" I muttered, checking my e-mail, then my texts. Was Meredith meeting friends after dinner? It was getting late.

By the time I'd cleaned up, Meredith and Allen sat in the living room. She stared at her laptop. Allen lounged in his chair with the remote control in his hand.

"Are you staying home tonight?" I asked Meredith.

"Hmm." She focused on the screen.

"Meredith, answer me."

She finally looked up. "Answer what?"

Allen sighed, changing the channel. "You're just like your mother," he grumbled. "You never listen."

"What are you talking about?" I asked.

Allen's face flushed. "It's true. When I'm trying to talk to you, you're always doing other things. You say 'Uh-huh,' but don't hear half of what I've said. Now, Meredith's doing it."

"I have to do several things at once to get everything done," I snapped. "Just because I'm not looking at you doesn't mean I don't hear you."

"You tune me out most of the time."

"We'll talk about this later."

But we didn't. We went to bed in a funk. Why didn't Allen get it? I was a busy person. I juggled work, home, motherhood, and elderly parents. I didn't have time to just listen. Lord, make Allen understand, I prayed. For all I knew, God was too busy to listen, too.

Soon afterwards, Allen and I happened to watch a motivational show on TV.

"Good communication is more than just sharing information," the speaker said. "You can clear up many misunderstandings by taking the time to listen." He paused and seemed to look straight at us. "Listening keeps you connected — an important part of intimacy."

Allen and I stared at each other for a moment, a little stunned at the timing of the show on listening.

"You're right," I said to him. "Sometimes I think I'm listening, but I'm not concentrating. I do care about you and what you're saying."

My confession opened the floodgates. We said what was on

our minds without distractions. And we both listened. No need for "What'd I say?"

That night as I said my prayers, I threw in, "Thanks for listening."

My Prayer

Dear Lord, help me really listen to show that I care. Remind me that paying close attention will make me a better wife and mother, and deepen my relationships with my loved ones.

Amen.

24

Any Salt for These Words?

By Linda Apple

My dear brothers and sisters, take note of this: Everyone should be quick to listen, slow to speak and slow to become angry...
~James 1:19

Several years ago, while visiting missionary friends in Yamaranguila, Honduras, I was only able to use the Internet every few days. One day, I had a message from my husband that said, "Declaring war on dust. Buying another vacuum cleaner. Also made you a budget. Will discuss when you get home."

The hairs rose on the back of my neck. Just exactly what was he saying? That I was a bad housekeeper? That I spent too much money? I thought about how hard I worked to keep our house clean, how I hardly had any clothes in my closet and three pairs of shoes to my name because I wouldn't spend money to get them. My slow burn erupted into full flame as I rapidly typed my response—more like a rebuttal.

Since I was leaving the next day for home, there wasn't time for me to get an answer from him, so I seethed on the jet and thought of all the other things I was going to say to him in setting things straight.

When he met me at the airport, I fixed my glare on him. He lifted his hands. "What was that answer all about?" I let him have it. He set me down and said, "Honey, all I was saying was that you needed better equipment. After using that old clunker of ours, I realized how hard it was for you to clean house. So, I bought you the best vacuum cleaner money could buy. And as for the budget, I rearranged things so you could have some spending money to buy clothes and things for yourself."

"Oh." I looked around for something to crawl under. I remembered the scripture that exhorted me to "be quick to listen, slow to speak and slow to become angry." How I wished I had done just that. I asked the Lord, and then my husband, to forgive me.

Since that day, I have taken James 1:19 to heart. When Neal says something that raises my defenses, I have learned to say, "This is what I hear you saying." Then I repeat what filtered through my mind. More often than not, his response is, "No, that isn't what I meant."

Admittedly, there are times when I ignore the wisdom in this scripture, and I always regret it. In the airport that day many years ago, I learned the hard way about the truth in the old saying: Make your words soft and sweet. You never know which ones you'll have to eat.

My Prayer

Lord, how often we jump to the wrong conclusion and make a mess of our lives and the lives of those we love. I pray that you will guard my tongue today so that I might be slow to speak. Fill me instead with your Holy Spirit and the wisdom that only comes from above.

Amen.

25

You Are Mine

By Carol Hatcher

I am my beloved's and my beloved is mine.
~Song of Songs 6:3

I wasn't sure what to say. I lay staring at this man I'd chosen. I wanted to express everything I felt with words. I wanted to tell him how I loved the way his hand fit in the small of my back and how sometimes he would close his giant hand over mine and kiss my knuckles. Maybe I could share how irresistible he was when he would kiss the tiny clips or barrettes I wore in my hair because he said they were so cute.

Perhaps I could make him understand how my insides felt when he broke into a full-blown smile. Or how I adored the way his voice lifted ever so slightly with anticipation when he answered the phone if I called him at work.

I wished our minds could meld so I could adequately express my sorrow for the times I took him for granted or snapped at him when my temper flared. My heart raced as I watched him breathe and noticed the stubble across his face. My fingers ached to touch that sandpapery skin.

I thought about how to make him understand the depth of my love — how I knew he was chosen for me. I listened to his steady breathing and realized even that brought me comfort.

Perhaps if I told him he was my best friend. But I'd claimed my girlfriends Mary Ann and Allison for years to fill that cherished role. The way I loved this man was even more than the role of a best friend. He was my partner, my lover, my shoulder, my heart.

I wiggled across the sheets, close enough to breathe him in. I walked my fingers up his chest and traced his lips. With no grand poem or collection of words, I said all that was in my soul.

"You're my favorite person," I sighed.

"And you are mine," he whispered as we drifted off to sleep.

My Prayer

Thank you, God, for the gift of my spouse. On the days when tensions rise and anger flares, help me remember the tender moments we've shared and to cherish this man.

Amen.

The Wake-Up Call

By Amy L. Stout

The LORD is compassionate and gracious, slow to anger, abounding in love.
~Psalm 103:8

I was in newlywed bliss! My husband and I had been married for a short time, and we loved sharing life together. We had moved far away from family and friends to be near my husband's military base, but it didn't matter to this smitten bride.

While my husband was learning how to effectively protect our country by mastering military tactics and parachuting from airplanes, I spent my days caring for our home, fixing elegant meals, and counting the minutes until we could be together again.

Our evenings were spent chatting over dinner, snuggling close while watching television, or holding hands while playing board games.

We enjoyed serving one another. Every morning at 4:30, in the chill of daybreak, I would get up and put my husband's clothes in the dryer so they would be toasty warm for him when he was ready to get dressed. At the end of every day, he would graciously rub the soreness from my feet.

Since I knew his job was dangerous, I chose to live as though every day were our last.

Because of our early rising, sleep would come quickly at the end of the day. But before we embarked on our journey to Dreamland, we would nestle close together like two spoons tucked in a drawer. My husband's strong arm would be under my head, and his chest would protectively wrap around my back for a cozy night's sleep.

One night in particular will forever be etched in my memory. We had been sleeping for a few hours when, all of a sudden, I felt pressure around my head and a squeezing around my neck. My husband, in a very deep sleep, was putting me in a chokehold! I was so shocked that not one word escaped my lips. Before I could recover from being nearly choked to death, my husband reeled back, and in full force head butted me!

At that point, I was fully awake and I screamed, "What are you doing?" My husband woke up and was horrified to find his arm cinched around my neck and a large bump emerging on my head.

My poor husband was inconsolable as he explained that he was having a dream where I was being attacked, and he had been trying to protect me from my assailant. He felt terrible that he had hurt me.

Two decades have gone by, and I still find myself reflecting on the lesson of that unfortunate and startling incident. From time to time in a marriage, we hurt each other. We don't intend to, and sometimes we aren't even aware that we have offended. Our compassion and forgiveness are essential to the preservation of a loving relationship. We need to be swift to forgive, to mend the relationship, and to express our sincere, heartfelt sorrow at hurting those we treasure.

My Prayer

*Dear Lord, sometimes we unknowingly harm
those we love with our words or deeds.
Please help us to quickly and humbly make
amends. Please polish away the tarnish that
threatens to dull our relationship and help
us to reflect your perfect example of love,
compassion, and forgiveness.*

Amen.

27

My Petri Dish Experiment

By DV Mason

But the wisdom that comes from heaven is first of all pure; then peace-loving,
considerate, submissive, full of mercy and good fruit, impartial and sincere.
Peacemakers who sow in peace reap a harvest of righteousness.
~James 3:17-18

I was a stay-at-home mother, and I loved that role. But being a wife, not so much. My husband and I never fought, but we didn't bring much joy to each other either.

While studying the book of James, I was asked to look up the word "peacemaker." I did it half-heartedly because, of course, I already knew what it meant: one who settles conflicts. But the study taught me that a peacemaker also *prevents* conflicts by creating peace in the first place. Wow! Now, that was a different challenge. It required me to monitor the words that came out of my mouth, the tone in which I spoke them, and my actions. I liked the first definition a whole lot better; I was pretty good at that one. I didn't score high on the "creating peace" definition.

My husband and I were leaving for Hawaii, just the two of us. It was the ideal opportunity to monitor everything I said. I called it my "petri dish experiment." A petri dish is used in research laboratories.

Often it's filled with a culture medium (Hawaii), contaminated in some way (by my tongue), and then the researcher (me) waits to see what grows.

In Hawaii, I claimed every opportunity to give my husband praise or to thank him. I stopped before speaking to evaluate whether my words were hurtful. I began to recognize how carelessly my words had slipped out in the past, and I was stunned by how easily they could wound instead of encourage. With intentional care, I chose words that exhorted. I discovered, much to my surprise, that I didn't always have to say the first thing that came to my mind. If I paused—and, believe me, that was hard to do—I could determine whether my words were true, necessary, and kind.

This went on for several days. I thought my husband would catch on and ask, "What's up with you?" He's an intelligent man, but he never caught on. By the end of the trip, he couldn't do enough for me. He had us biking down a volcano and snorkeling, two things we'd never done on past visits. I'm an outdoor girl, so he did these things for me.

My carefully chosen words created a miracle before my eyes. My precious husband grew taller. He stood straighter. He shined. My petri dish of praise and exhortation produced a happier husband.

I wish I could look back on that experiment as a complete victory. And to the extent that I learned an important lesson, it was—a big one. But part of the lesson was one of shame and sadness. All those years, all those chances to build him up... what would have happened if I'd done my part better? All I could do about the past was ask for forgiveness and change my ways for the future.

Now, the children are gone and it's just the two of us. We've discovered joy in each other. My petri dish of peace-producing words grew a healthier, happier marriage.

My Prayer

Lord, may the words that I speak be chosen
by you. Give me, I pray, insight into the effect
of my words before I speak them.

Amen.

28

Crowning, Not Crippling, My Husband

By Marcia Hornok

Set a guard over my mouth, LORD; keep watch over the door of my lips.
~Psalm 141:3

"How long have you two been married?" I asked the couple sitting across the table from us.

"Forty-six years."

"You are to be commended," my husband Ken said.

This couple was new in our community and had visited our church that morning, so we invited them out to eat with us. In the course of our conversation, it became apparent that the wife did most of the talking. Her husband would start to answer a question we posed, but the wife would finish his sentence or correct what he said. I'm sure she was aiming for accuracy, but this habit did more harm than good.

Then I mentally pointed a finger at myself. I frequently did that to Ken, even though he was a pastor and good at public speaking.

When I answered for him, clarified his stories, or rolled my eyes at his jokes, I diminished his self-confidence.

I thought of the proverb that said, "A wife of noble character is her husband's crown, but a disgraceful wife is like decay in his bones" (Proverbs 12:4). Instead of being a crown to Ken, I tried to be his crutch, which he didn't need. I was making him feel like a cripple, not a king. Like the wife in the restaurant, I was not intentionally trying to disgrace my husband — I was trying to be helpful — but we made our husbands feel inadequate as conversationalists.

Communication is the backbone of marriage. I felt like Ken and I were already practicing good conversation habits with each other at home. When I had something to tell him, he would give me his full attention, even muting the TV if he was watching it. Likewise, I would stop what I was doing and look at him when he talked to me. If he complained about circumstances beyond my control, I knew he needed sympathy, not solutions, so I tried not to contradict him.

Yet in public I wanted the spotlight to shine on me. I consider myself a fast thinker, and being more decisive than Ken, I often blurted out answers before he had a chance to speak. However, Ken usually had wiser and more objective responses if I only waited for them.

I knew what I needed to do — retrain myself, with God's help. Now when someone asks us a question, I try to remember not to cripple Ken. By silently calling on God to guard my mouth, I am learning to wait for Ken's answer. That's how I can be a wife of noble character and treat him royally.

My Prayer

Lord, help me to honor my husband in social situations by not speaking for him or contradicting what he says. Enable me to crown him with respect and admiration.

Amen.

29

A Tank of Gasoline and Grace

By Andrea B. Fortenberry

Therefore, as God's chosen people, holy and dearly loved, clothe yourselves with compassion, kindness, humility, gentleness and patience. Bear with each other and forgive one another if any of you has a grievance against someone. Forgive as the Lord forgave you.
~Colossians 3:12-13

On our second Easter as a married couple, we drove to meet my family for a picnic after church. I knew our car was low on gas. I had mentioned it to my husband the day before. But he had been tired of my nagging lately, so I thought I'd wait and see if he'd notice that the warning light was on.

We got about five miles from our house when the car started sputtering and died. He pulled over and got out of the car. I wanted to yell, "I told you we needed gas!" Instead, I offered to call roadside assistance. The wait would be more than an hour, an eternity for an angry wife who was biting her tongue.

Thankfully, we didn't have to wait that long as numerous people stopped to assist us. We accepted the help of a family who took my husband for gas. While I waited with the car, I thought it over and decided not to say "I told you so." Why further ruin our Easter? Why place blame and make my husband feel bad, when that's the last thing I'd want him to do to me?

He returned with the gas and poured it into the tank. We drove away a few minutes later. We were a little late to our Easter picnic that day, but it turned out to be for our benefit.

This lesson in grace has served us well in our nine years of marriage. There have been numerous instances, some minor and others major, when I could have torn down my husband for mistakes he's made. And there have been many opportunities for him to do the same to me. I'm not always perfect, but I try to respond with grace and mercy instead of blame and condemnation. It's how I want my husband to respond to me.

It's through these mess-ups, mistakes and disappointments of married life that God reveals His grace to us and through us. Grace is not deserved, but an unmerited gift of love from the giver. When I extend grace to my husband, I'm reminded of the grace that God extends to me and how much I need it.

My Prayer

Lord, we know that in marriage, we will
make mistakes and hurt one another. During
these times, please help us to respond to our
husbands as you respond to us—with honor,
love and grace. Help us to be a reflection
of you as we walk together in this gift and
journey of marriage.

Amen.

30

A Lesson in the Coffee Aisle

By Linda Mehus-Barber

"But the things that come out of a person's mouth come from the heart..."
~Matthew 15:18

The old man in the coffee aisle dawdled along, his head drooping slightly as he eyed the vast array of choices in front of him. He grimaced at the sound of his wife's voice. "Will you hurry up? You'd think by now you'd know what kind of coffee we get." He reached out and pulled a green package off the shelf, then shuffled over and handed the bag to his wife. She took one glance, and her mocking tone was like a slap. "Stupid, this is regular grind. We use fine grind. Go back and get the blue one."

I wanted to reach out and hug the old man. I wanted to say to his wife, "How could you be so cruel?" But of course I didn't. I just thought to myself how glad I was that I wasn't a nag like that.

My shopping done, I headed home. Loading up the bags of groceries in my arms, I staggered to the door and kicked it open. I heaved a huge sigh as I let them drop to the floor. My husband, stretched out on the recliner watching TV, sat up. "Oh, I should have come out to help you."

"Yes, that would have been nice," I responded and turned to put away the groceries. Nursing resentment, I made sure the cupboard doors banged as I opened and closed them. The "ouch" I muttered when I bumped into a misplaced chair was louder than need be. And as I started cooking supper, I groaned audibly every time I had to move jars to get at something in the over-crowded fridge.

There wasn't much conversation as we ate on TV tables. As usual, I wished we could eat at a regular table like regular people do. As I prepared to wash the dishes, Don grabbed a dishtowel and started to tease me. I don't remember what I said, and nor does he, but whatever it was, it went into his spirit like a dagger. The look on his face was like that of the old man in the coffee aisle.

"Is that what you really think?" he choked out.

"Oh, I didn't mean it. I was just joking," I quipped back.

He looked at me, and his words stung because I knew they were true. "You wouldn't say it if it wasn't in your heart."

That night, I saw a bit of the old man's wife in me, and I prayed for God to show me how to love my husband. These days, I try to bite my tongue when criticism sits on the tip of it and to speak words of encouragement more often. Because of a chance encounter in the coffee aisle and my husband's courage to speak the truth to me, God has started to change me. In the process, my husband is enjoying the freedom to become the kind of man God meant him to be.

My Prayer

Lord, open my eyes to see the truth in my ways, and may I have the willingness to change as you direct. May I be a wife whose words build up so that my husband can have the confidence to become all that you intend him to be.

Amen.

I Am a Skeksis

By Dena Harris

Sarah said, "God has brought me laughter, and everyone who hears about this will laugh with me."
~Genesis 21:6

My husband of sixteen years and I were in the car, driving home after doing a bit of shopping. We'd been chatting about work and family when I turned to him and asked, "So, how are we doing?"

It's hard to explain the grimace of pain that contorts my husband's face whenever I utter this simple phrase. For me, the question is a simple way of checking in, like opening the oven door a crack to see how the roast is cooking. My husband, however, greets the inquiry as though he's just been through a welcome session at Guantanamo.

"We're fine. I'm fine! Everything is fine! No, not fine. Great! We're great! Why?" (And here his face contorted in another clenched-teeth grimace.) "What do you think is wrong?"

"I don't think anything is wrong," I replied.

"Oh, yes, you do. The only time you ask how we're doing is when you have something to say about how we're doing, and it's something that you think is a problem. Or I'm doing something wrong. So just go ahead and tell me what it is, and I'll stop doing it. Or start doing it. Or whatever."

"Nothing's wrong!" I said. "I was just checking in to make sure you were happy with how we we're doing…"

"I'm always happy with how we are. I'm a man. I don't know any better."

"…and to give you the opportunity to say something, if something needed to be said. Because that's what a thoughtful and caring wife like me does." I gave him a pointed look.

He patted my leg. "I'm sorry. It's just that you have a little Skeksis in you."

"Excuse me?" I asked.

"You know, the Skeksis from that '80s movie, *The Dark Crystal*."

"Ye-ss," I said cautiously.

"Well, remember the scene where the main Skeksis approached the Gelflings, Jen and Kira, in the forest and he said, 'Skeksis friend! Stay! Skeksis friend with Gelfling!' Okay, so you knew he was lying or had ulterior motives. That's you, honey."

"Just to be clear," I said, "I'm trying to improve our relationship through open communication, and your response to that is to compare me to a large, badly dressed turkey buzzard from a Jim Henson movie?"

"See?" said my husband. "Right there. Total Skeksis attitude."

"I don't think other couples have conversations like this," I said.

"You're welcome," he replied.

He has a point. Routine breeds boredom. After sixteen years of marriage, I still never know what's going to come out of his mouth. It's part of the fun of being married to him.

Even if he does call me a Skeksis.

My Prayer

Lord, may love and laughter light my days for many years to come. Continue to bless my marriage and help me remember to cherish the good times always.

Amen.

32

Learning to Slow Down

By Marilyn Turk

...so that you may live a life worthy of the Lord and please him in every way: bearing fruit in every good work, growing in the knowledge of God, being strengthened with all power according to his glorious might so that you may have great endurance and patience...
~Colossians 1:10-11

"Hello! I'm home!" As I entered the back door, I announced my arrival and waited for my husband's response.

Silence. I roamed through the house, curious as to why he didn't answer. When I spotted the back of his head as he sat on the sofa in front of the TV, my anger reflex began to kick in. So, was this what he'd been doing since I left this morning?

The kitchen table was still covered with paperwork he was supposed to do. A glance at the back yard revealed the de-robed Christmas tree waiting to be taken to the street. I wanted to ask what he'd been doing and why he hadn't done those things. I was in high gear, anxious for results, and here he sat, doing nothing. Chuck was seldom in a hurry, but now that he'd retired, he seemed to have slowed down even more.

But something inside told me to keep my mouth shut. After all, I didn't want to come in the house and start berating him.

"Chuck?" He hadn't moved yet, so I thought perhaps he'd dozed off.

At last, he turned and said, "Oh, hi. I didn't hear you come in. I was eating lunch."

Okay, it was lunchtime. That's fair. I decided to suppress my irritation and let it go. As the day progressed, I discovered what he had done while I was gone.

"I put air in your bike tires."

"You did? Thanks."

I noticed the bird feeder was full. "You refilled the bird-feeder? Thanks!"

"I put those boxes in the attic."

"Oh. Good."

Plus, he'd been working on our taxes, a chore I was grateful he took on.

As it turned out, he had accomplished several things while I was gone. Boy, was I glad I had kept my mouth shut.

Since we got married four years ago, I've come to realize our differences. I'm quick to react, jump to conclusions, and give a hasty reply. Chuck, on the other hand, is slow to answer, analytical and chooses his words carefully. At first, it bothered me when I wanted a swift response. But now I appreciate the way he does things—thoroughly, well thought-out, carefully researched.

Those attributes have come in handy for me. When I'm frustrated with my computer, Chuck will calmly take over and figure out the problem, relieving me of my anxiety. Instruction manuals and bookkeeping tasks stress me out, but Chuck doesn't mind taking the time to examine and understand them. I am thankful for his slowness, or should I say patience, in those matters.

The Bible says, "Everyone should be quick to listen, slow to speak and slow to become angry" (James 1:19). Chuck gets it, and I need to follow his example.

My Prayer

Lord, please slow me down when I'm too
quick to react the wrong way. Help me listen
with an open heart and follow your pure
example. Father, I ask for continued blessings
for my family.

Amen.

33

Grace and Peace

By Mary W. Bridgman

Grace and peace to you from God our Father and from the Lord Jesus Christ.
~Romans 1:7b

I knew there wasn't enough room for my husband to make the turn he was attempting in a cramped restaurant parking lot. He'd originally planned to park across the street, but I thought I spotted a space in the parking lot near the front door. I was wrong, so Ben decided to turn around. I yelped when I heard an ominous grinding noise beneath the floorboards. Ben kept going until it stopped. After we parked and inspected the car, we realized he'd driven over an ornamental rock bordering the pavement.

I gritted my teeth and thought, "If he'd just backed up before he turned around, he would have missed the rock." But knowing it was my suggestion that sent him into the lot in the first place, I kept my mouth shut.

Ben was unusually quiet during dinner. I knew he was upset by the damage to our car and probably felt foolish for having caused it. Later, as he drove us home, I turned toward him. Feeling somewhat magnanimous because I hadn't given in to my earlier impulse to criticize his decision to turn the car around in a small space, I said, "I don't want you to be upset about the car. It's not worth the worry; it could just as easily have happened to me."

Before we went to bed that evening, Ben thanked me for being so understanding. Suddenly, I realized he had done the same thing for me many years earlier. I had backed into a post in a cramped parking lot. Without complaint or one word of reproach, Ben took the car to the body shop and paid to have it repaired. As I recalled the incident, the glow of pride I felt due to my generosity toward Ben seemed to lose a little of its luster.

I remembered how often Ben had shown grace—especially kindness and mercy—to me during the fifteen years of our marriage. So many times, when I apologized for something I had said or done, he would say he had already forgotten about it. Ben's continuing grace toward me brings to mind the phrase employed by the apostle Paul in his letters to the early churches, "Grace and peace to you from God our Father and from the Lord Jesus Christ."

Grace begets grace, and the ultimate result is peace—peace in our hearts, peace in our relationships, and peace in our homes.

My Prayer

*Lord, thank you for the grace and peace that
you impart so freely to me. May I share it
with all those whom you place in my path,
but first and foremost with my beloved
husband, who is so gracious and kind to me.*

Amen.

Letting Go of the Grapes

By Shawnelle Eliasen

Therefore encourage one another and build each other up,
just as in fact you are doing.
~1 Thessalonians 5:11

My husband and I sat on the back patio. The air hung August-hot. I held my iced tea glass against my neck. The cubes had melted, but the glass was still cool.

"It's nice," my husband Lonny said, "to sit for a minute."

He looked toward our aboveground pool. Our five sons splashed and shouted.

"It is," I said. "Here. Have some fruit."

I'd made a big platter for the kids. There were strawberries. Sliced kiwi. Chunks of pineapple. And clusters of crisp, cold grapes.

"Thanks," he said.

I admired his strong jaw. His blue eyes. The way the sun had warmed his skin. Life was good. Sitting here. With him. In the August heat. Listening to the play of our offspring with the only man I've loved.

Lonny grabbed a bunch of purple grapes.

And I cringed.

Lonny has a way of eating grapes. I'm not sure why, but if they're crisp, the sound just echoes in his head. It's loud. It's crunchy. He's not smacking. His mouth is closed. He's polite. But the sound is unnerving. It grates at me. It grates my nerves raw until all I see is red.

Lonny smiled. "Love you," he said, oblivious to the racket that resounded from his head. He reached for another bunch of grapes. Popped one in his mouth. The snapping and popping and chewing began.

I opened my mouth to say something about whatever wild thing happened in his head with the grapes.

But he smiled again. And I looked at my man. My good man. My take-care-of-the-family man. My thoughtful, honest, strong, love-the-Lord man. And the grape sound paled against his goodness.

"I love you, too," I said.

And I meant it.

Sometimes loving means letting go. Letting go of criticism.

And letting go of the grapes.

My Prayer

*Lord, thank you for this kind, dear man.
Soften my heart to allow your Holy Spirit to
enter my soul when unkind words threaten
my lips. Help me to use only words that
build him up and create an everlasting bond
between us.*

Amen.

Chapter
4

Devotional Stories for Wives

Embracing Our Differences

We have different gifts, according to the grace given to each of us.

~Romans 12:6

The Two Shall Become One

By Donna Teti

By the seventh day God had finished the work he had been doing;
so on the seventh day he rested from all his work. Then God blessed the
seventh day and made it holy, because on it he rested from all the work
of creating that he had done.
~Genesis 2:2-3

"Hon, come on! You promised to be ready!" I yelled to my husband, Marc, trying to hide the irritation in my voice. "We should have left ten minutes ago for the party!" I looked out the window. Marc had not even begun to clean up. The wheelbarrow filled with dirt was still there as he continued to work with the rake in our vegetable garden.

"Sorry, hon, just a few more minutes," he answered, oblivious to my annoyance. Every weekend, it was the same. Marc was up at the crack of dawn on Saturdays with projects lined up for the whole weekend.

Not me! My weekdays were filled with laundry, cooking, food shopping, cleaning, and driving the kids back and forth to activities. When the weekend came, I wanted to relax and have some fun! As the kids got older, there were less chores, but I still looked forward to weekends when I could unwind with a good book or a long nap!

Marc found my naps as annoying as I found his mile-long list of things to do. He would just be ready to turn the music up full volume while he painted a door or washed the car when I would announce, "I'm going to take a little nap!" The music was lowered, but I could see the aggravation in his eyes. Many times, we ended up arguing over his projects and my naps, and how we should spend our weekends.

Through the years, we prayed often. Please, God, help us to stop arguing over this! Help him/her to see my point of view!

I'd like to say change came quickly, but it did not... it was a slow process. Yet as we both continued to pray and work hard at our marriage, God opened our eyes, and we began to appreciate how each of us enjoyed our weekends in different ways.

Now, I often find Marc taking a break on the back porch to read a chapter from a book or magazine. Other times, he finds me joyfully surrounded by flats of zinnias and snapdragons on a Saturday afternoon, completely engaged in a gardening project.

But I knew we had changed a lot when we were heading to a family party this past weekend. "What time do you want to go, dear?" Marc asked.

"Well, Bill said any time after 3:00, but I'd like to finish washing this kitchen floor first. How about 4:30?" I answered.

"That's great!" Marc smiled. "That will give me just enough time to sneak in a little nap."

My Prayer

*Father, help us remember that change
sometimes comes slowly, but is just as fruitful
when it finally comes. Thank you for giving
me a husband who works so hard taking
care of our home. Continue to show me
your compassion as I continue to honor my
husband in all my thoughts and deeds.*

Amen.

Meatloaf for My Man

By Shawnelle Eliasen

On this mountain the LORD Almighty will prepare a feast of rich food for all peoples, a banquet of aged wine — the best of meats and the finest of wines.
~Isaiah 25:6

"Do I smell meatloaf?" my husband Lonny asked. His eyes were bright and hopeful. When he placed his bag on the kitchen floor and walked to the dining room, I think there was a bounce in his step.

"No, sorry," I said. I placed napkins around our long family table. "It's quiche. But it's a new recipe. I think you'll like it."

Lonny slid his arm around my waist, and his lips grazed my cheek. "Okay," he said. "But I wish it were meatloaf."

"I know," I said. "Poor, sweet man. Maybe you'll strike it rich another night."

Sometimes, I like to kid Lonny about his affection for meatloaf. The man just loves it. Trouble is, no one else in the house shares his affinity. Lonny and I have five sons, and they're hearty eaters, easy to please. But not one of them has even the most miniscule appreciation for a morsel of meatloaf. Even I don't get excited about it. My grandfather used to make a mean one, but that was years ago, and I don't have his recipe. Plus, I'm a writer, and the word "meatloaf," in my opinion, leaves a little to be desired.

So we rarely feast on a loaf of meat.

Dinnertime came that evening, and we gathered around the table. I sliced the quiche and handed Lonny his plate.

And as his hands reached out, as we curled our hands around the same plate, something inside me went soft.

Lonny's had a lot on his shoulders lately. He's learning a new job at age forty-five. He's coaching two basketball teams for our smaller sons. One of our teenage boys is dishing out a fair amount of grief. And Lonny, my stable, dependable, no-frills man, takes it all in stride.

"The man deserves a meatloaf," I decided as I dished up another serving of quiche.

The next night, Lonny came home and dropped his bag in the kitchen. "Do I smell meatloaf?" he said.

"Sure do," I said.

Lonny wrapped his arms around me tight. It would be worth a few grumbles, this smile that stretched over my husband's dear face.

And making him so happy was pretty simple, after all. All I had to do was to serve "a seasoned rectangular brick of beef."

My Prayer

*Father, thank you that I can please my
husband in such small, simple ways. Help me
remember to offer these gifts with a willing
heart and a ready smile.*

Amen.

37

A Déjà Vu Moment

By Diane Buller

May our Lord Jesus Christ himself and God our Father,
who loved us and by his grace gave us eternal encouragement
and good hope, encourage your hearts and strengthen you
in every good deed and word.
~2 Thessalonians 2:16-17

"You want to do what?" I took a breath and leaned up against the stainless steel kitchen sink. I had married a man who didn't brainstorm about his career plans. "But isn't that 100% commission?" I knew the answer before I asked. "But the timing isn't good. We have two preschoolers, a mortgage, a car payment, not enough savings…" I sighed.

"I'm tired of climbing the corporate ladder. I'm tired of commuting an hour twice a day. And I don't want to be told when we'll move and where we'll live." My husband's words trailed off.

I pleaded. I begged. We negotiated. Why did the words "challenge" and "risk" energize my husband, yet instill fear in me? Why did all my questions begin with "But…?" Why did most of our big discussions seem to take place at the kitchen sink? One question replaced another.

The next day, I called my dad and shared both sides as fairly as I could. "Opportunity never comes at an opportune time," Dad replied matter-of-factly.

"Oh, great!" I muttered, as I hung up the phone. Even my dad was on his side!

I whined. I cried. I lay awake at night. Then I prayed. And prayed. It was the classic conflict: Man vs. Himself. Or, in this case, Wife vs. Herself. Finally, thoughts of "Why would he do this *to* us?" shifted to "Why would he do this *for* us?" Hadn't he shared his desire to "be his own boss" when we dated? Hadn't I also been dreading another move... again?

Nights later, I lay awake again. Praying more. *Let him live his dream.* The words were not my own. I took a breath, got out of bed and walked downstairs where he was reading. Standing in front of him, I spoke three words, "Let's do it!"

Twenty years later, the nest is empty. I look out my kitchen window above a stainless steel sink in a different house across town. I daydream. Balancing lesson plans and grading, home and writing leave me conflicted. I want to stay home and write. But we still have one in college. And there is that familiar emotion... fear! I lie awake at night. I pray.

"The timing isn't good!" I say to my husband.

"I understand. And I'll support you." His soft words speak hope and encouragement to my fearful heart. That déjà vu moment would carry me to the next step. The rest would come from above.

My Prayer

Dear God, please help me to support my husband when he shares his dreams with me. May I always be open to the possibilities that await us, rather than the obstacles in our path. I trust that you will see us through whatever new journeys we embark on together.

Amen.

38

Hooked

By Sherrie Murphree

Do nothing out of selfish ambition or vain conceit. Rather, in humility
value others above yourselves, not looking to your own interests but each
of you to the interests of the others.
~Philippians 2:3-4

I'm a city gal who didn't fish growing up. My country-boy husband forgot to ask if I liked fishing before we wed. For Mel's sake, it would have been good if I liked fishing, but for years, any way I could I wormed out of it.

One day in a public testimony at church, a lady mentioned that speaking was not her comfort zone but she was trying it anyway. God seemed to dangle His lure before me to wiggle out of my comfort zone. I needed to try fishing.

The three significant people in Mel's life who had fished with him—his dad, his brother, and our son—had died within a three-year span, so I had been praying for a new fishing partner for Mel. Now I felt a nudge from God to be that partner myself.

One Saturday, we went shopping at Sears and dropped by the sporting goods department. A salesman approached and said, "Good afternoon. We're having a drawing for fishing equipment. Be sure to register the next aisle over."

"You go ahead and look around, Mel. I'll sign up for both of us," I volunteered.

Back home, we listened to our answering machine. "This message is for a Mrs. Murphree. You've won a combo rod and reel in our Sears drawing. We'll hold it for you."

At once, we returned to claim the prize. "A light Shakespeare combo. That's just what you need, Sherrie," Mel encouraged. But with raised eyebrows, I recalled Shakespeare only through literature courses. We thanked Sears and left.

At Walmart the next week, I decided impulsively to buy a fishing license. But even waiting in line five minutes seemed too long. How could I be patient enough for fishing?

One mild September morning, I agreed to go to Moss Creek Lake to fish. The excursion was tolerable, although only a turtle pulled on my line. Time passed quickly as I worked on my casting and reeling skills. For Mel's sake, I tried hard. When I asked the difference between lures and bait, he proved to be as good a teacher as a fisherman. Ominous clouds got me off the hook a couple of hours early as rain began.

Three weeks later, we went fishing again. Perfect day. From the dock I worked on my angler skills once more. When I did well, Mel praised, "Hey, that was a good one!" When my line got tangled, he sympathized. "That's okay. I'll just cut it." I had several catfish bites this time.

Eventually, the day arrived when I was compelled to admit something to Mel. "You know, I'm actually enjoying this fishing some." He let out a chuckle.

Time would tell if fishing would become a new comfort zone for me. I was learning to feel the thrill of a fish tugging on the end of my line. I was responding to God's pull on my heart, the one that had started in church that long ago day.

"Reel me in, Lord," I whispered.

My Prayer

Father, help me to learn the joy of participating in my husband's delights. Give me the courage to step out of my comfort zone so that we may share new and fun experiences together.

Amen.

"I caught more than a fish this weekend... I caught a happy marriage!"

Reprinted by permission of
Stephanie Piro ©2013

39

Harmony in Marriage

By Sheri Zeck

Finally, all of you, be like-minded, be sympathetic, love one another, be
compassionate and humble.
~1 Peter 3:8

I folded my arms and stared out the car's passenger window. I couldn't believe this one simple question still caused conflict between my husband and me: What do you want to do this weekend?

I'll admit Curt's outgoing personality was one of the qualities I first liked about him. He could talk to anyone, even the stranger standing behind him in the grocery store checkout line. But after we got married, our personality differences became a real problem. Time and again, Curt's desire to socialize clashed with my need for a peaceful evening at home. Now, here we were again, on our way to a party I'd rather not attend.

A popular song from our dating days broke the tension. I turned up the radio and tapped my foot to the lively beat. Curt drummed his fingers against the steering wheel. Before long, we were singing together.

At the chorus, I switched to a higher pitch and harmonized with Curt as he sang the melody. The song sounded even better. We blend together pretty well, I thought. Two different parts added a richness that one voice couldn't achieve.

As we continued singing, my mind drifted back to our argument. If only we could blend that well in our marriage. Curt and I were so different.

Then, suddenly, it hit me. That's how God intended it to be in marriage! God made us different by design. Though our differences sometimes created tension, God knew we'd be better together.

Over time, I started thinking of my marriage like that song. Instead of clashing with my husband, I looked for ways I could blend with him. Instead of arguing with him, I tried understanding him.

We now see how our differences have made us more effective as a couple than we ever could have been individually. Maybe I needed a little push to join the rest of the world. And I think Curt has realized a quiet evening at home isn't so bad after all.

After almost twenty years of marriage, we are learning to appreciate our differences. We're getting better at blending, and our marriage is more beautiful today because we each add our part.

My Prayer

Father, thank you for giving me your special gift: my husband. Help me examine my own attitude and selfish motives when it comes to my marriage. Give me a greater capacity to understand, accept, and even appreciate our differences.

Amen.

40

Love One Another Deeply

By Sarah Bergman

...love one another deeply, from the heart.
~1 Peter 1:22

Our happy marriage floated along on its merry way for about five years, until one devastating fact became clear: We couldn't conceive. This led to specialists, years of graphing and temperature taking, painful and expensive tests, and a roller coaster of emotions as we got our hopes up each month only to have them dashed. Through it all, we poured out our hearts to God and each other. Ron was solid as a rock, supporting me through everything. Finally, we tearfully accepted that it might not be in God's plan for us to have a biological child. We started looking into adoption, but that didn't seem to be God's plan either.

Once we submitted to His will, God provided a miracle. Her name is Jennifer. We sailed right through my pregnancy in a cloud of happiness, never worrying about the challenges that lay ahead. Once the baby was born, and the euphoria wore off, we began to sense the beginning of an issue that would challenge our marriage many times over. We were so focused on *having* a baby, that we hardly ever discussed *raising* one.

We quickly found that our ideas of childrearing were vastly different. To sum it up, I expected Ron to be just like my dad, and he expected to be just like his dad. Never were there two more different types of fathers. Mine bragged about how much time he logged walking the floor with us when we were infants. He was involved in every aspect of our lives. He hugged us frequently, and to this day, tells us he loves us every time we talk. Ron's dad was in the military and travelled much of the time. His own father, Ron's grandfather, was a very hands-off and inexpressive father. Ron's father never told his kids he loved them, nor did he hug and kiss them, although he did love them and showed that love in other ways. In his view, the man was the provider, and the childrearing was left mostly to the wife. This issue ignited many arguments between us as our expectations collided.

This is not a dramatic story with a change-your-life moment. As with most marital issues, we had to learn to listen to each other, communicate clearly, and take all our problems to our Heavenly Father. Over time, Ron realized he wanted to be much more involved in his children's early lives than his father had been in his. His daughter quickly won over his heart, and he began to enjoy coaxing smiles and giggles out of her. He never enjoyed feeding or burping her, or changing diapers, but he did it when necessary.

I realized that I could not expect Ron to act like my own father. I had to start enjoying Ron's own wonderful, God-given qualities. We prayed together, argued often, and loved each other deeply. We learned to compromise as our family grew.

Our children are now teenagers, and although I'm sure we've made lots of mistakes along the way, our kids know they are deeply loved. Ron is a loving, caring father who supports and encourages them, and they are blessed to have two very different grandfathers who also love them deeply in their own special and unique ways. My love and admiration for my husband has grown so much as we've worked together to help each other be the best parents we can be.

My Prayer

Dear Father, please help us as we seek to love our children deeply and parent them in ways that glorify you. I ask for the strength, courage and love to shape them while resting in the knowledge that you alone are always ultimately in control of their lives.

Amen.

41

Man's Best Friend

By Susan Barclay

"What no eye has seen, what no ear has heard, and what no human mind has conceived—the things God has prepared for those who love him..."
~1 Corinthians 2:9

efore David and I married, the fact that he didn't love dogs as much as I did didn't really bother me. A future without a canine companion seemed a small price to pay to have this great guy in my life, and there was always a chance he might reconsider. It wasn't so much that David didn't like dogs, but that he hadn't grown up with them. And even though the feeling wasn't mutual, it was obvious that animals adored him.

Fast forward. Our teenage children have wanted a dog for eons, but David steadfastly refuses. "I know what will happen. They'll promise to look after it, and I'll be the one who's stuck."

I can hardly argue. When Annika and Kenneth were younger, we got them a guinea pig. They assured us they would look after Chewy, but when the novelty wore off, David and I became her primary caregivers. How would a dog be different? Anyway, "no dog" was part of our unspoken marriage "contract." I prayed about it from time to time, but never with great persistence.

I was surprised then when David began to mellow. "We can get a dog when the kids move out," he offered. I was hopeful but sad. Why deprive Annika and Kenneth of one of childhood's joys when they were already on the brink of adulthood?

Then, on summer vacation, driving down a road that wasn't on our original itinerary, I saw a sign. "Boston Terrier puppies for sale," I read aloud as we got closer.

We had already passed the driveway when David asked, "Want to stop and look?"

Well, since you ask!

David turned around and pulled up beside the house. Three adult Bostons and two puppies came bounding up. They showered us with doggy kisses. While we spoke with the breeder, I scooped up one of the pups, a cute and quiet little guy. The breeder suggested we take him back to our campground to "try him out."

The rest is history. Jazz quickly designated David his favorite person in the entire universe, and we adopted him the next day. Two years later, he is an integral member of our family, and the kids do their part to take care of him. He has been a blessing not only to me and our teenagers, but to David as well. Jazz is always happy to see him at the end of a long day, and whether David needs to burn off some energy or take a nap, he can count on his canine buddy to be at his side.

I won't guarantee that God will give you everything you want if you just wait long enough, or submit to your spouse patiently enough, but I do think it gives Him pleasure to honor the desires of your heart—from time to time, for His own reasons. Trust that God knows what is best for you and wait on Him. His plans for you are good.

My Prayer

Lord, sometimes it's hard to be patient. Help me to be thankful for all the blessings you have given me. Help me to trust that you know best, and to accept that sometimes your answer is "no" or "not right now." Teach me to be still so I can hear your voice.

Amen.

"I haven't changed my mind about dogs. I just happen to love this one!"

Reprinted by permission of
Stephanie Piro ©2013

Cooking for Two

By Emily Weaver

Then God said, "I give you every seed-bearing plant on the face of the
whole earth and every tree that has fruit with seed in it.
They will be yours for food."
~Genesis 1:29

Being a new wife means figuring out how to feed your new husband. It's not always easy, and from what I've seen, is the cause of much newlywed angst. When I was a new wife, I had to face the uncomfortable fact that while my husband was a wonderful, kind and caring man, he was also the pickiest eater I'd ever encountered.

I don't know why it bothered me so much. Why couldn't he eat peppers or bananas or tuna? It's not like he was allergic to them; he was just being a baby. Even so, I dutifully cooked him dinners that did not contain anything to offend his delicate taste buds. But as the weeks and months wore on, I became increasingly irritated.

One day as I sat at the kitchen table clipping coupons, it all came to a head. None of the coupons in the paper were for any products I'd normally buy, and yet I knew that if I couldn't find some coupons to shave a few dollars off our weekly grocery budget, I'd be in trouble come dinnertime. I was annoyed because the pasta sauce coupon I was eyeing was for a favorite product of mine that contained mushrooms and onions. I loved mushrooms and onions, but my husband did not. Was I really at the mercy of a man who wouldn't eat mushrooms and onions? Would I ever eat mushrooms and onions again? Why did God make me fall in love with someone who would turn his nose up at mushrooms and onions? How many other things was I going to have to forgo?

My husband must have seen me crying into the Sunday inserts because suddenly I felt a hand on my back.

"What's wrong?" he asked. "Why are you crying?"

I put my head on his shoulder and sobbed. I told him he was a hard man to cook for, and I thought I was supposed to enjoy that wifely duty. His pickiness was making me resent him, and I felt guilty. It wasn't that I didn't love him, I told him, but sometimes it would be nice to make something for dinner that I wanted, and not worry that he'd be upset or wouldn't eat.

"Listen," he said. "You didn't give yourself to me... God gave us to each other. We are bound into one. That means if you put me first, I put you first." Then he picked up the pasta coupon and said, "I can pick out mushrooms and onions with a fork. You don't have to give up your favorite pasta sauce."

Since that day, our pasta sauce has always contained mushrooms and onions. I do him a favor by supplying a little plate onto which he puts the offensive items, and then he returns the favor by pouring them into my pasta. Nothing like double mushrooms and onions to remind you that taking care of your husband often means he takes double care of you.

My Prayer

Lord, thank you for helping me to recognize
that even little differences between my
husband and me can drive a wedge between
us. Help us to handle these irritations with
compromise and humor.

Amen.

God Appears in Our Stillness

By Marijo Herndon

He says, "Be still, and know that I am God…"
~Psalm 46:10

Patience hasn't always been one of my virtues. I do most things quickly, and I expect others to do so, too. "Are you done yet?" "Are we there yet?" and "How long will it take?" are on my list of favorite things to say. Enjoying the journey has never been something I was good at. My eyes are always on the next thing to do, or the next place to go, or the next person to meet.

However, I married a man who has the patience of a saint. My husband is the type of person who can savor the moment. When we're vacationing at the ocean, I can look at the waves for a few minutes and then say, "Okay, let's do something else," while my husband can sit and enjoy the magnitude of the vast water for hours.

One day, while in Maine, we were sitting in our car, looking out at the ocean and watching the seagulls swoop up and down over the beach. One of them landed on the hood of our car and stared at me. We could see people in neighboring cars throwing bread to the other birds, but we didn't have any food. I couldn't understand why that seagull would have chosen to land on our car. And I certainly didn't know why he would look at me the way he did. He sat there for forty-five minutes, never taking his eyes off of me or moving a feather. I was so entertained by him.

Later that day, my husband told me that he had prayed something would keep me there, peacefully, in that car. He asked God to show me something that would make me slow down and just enjoy the day.

After years of marriage, I finally get him. I understand why he loves to linger on something for a long time. There is peace in each moment. There is God in that quietness. In those ordinary, simple pleasures, there is an extraordinary pay-off. I can hear my own thoughts, enjoy the presence of my husband in that stillness, and feel God's presence between us.

I've noticed that I don't experience God's best when I'm on the run. I don't feel His peace like I do when I'm just sitting with the man I gave my life to twenty-five years ago. I've learned to slow down, relish every moment, and be more like my husband, who taught me what God had in store all along.

My Prayer

*Lord, always make me grateful for the restful,
quiet times in our marriage. Please help me
to see you in the simple pleasures of each day.*

Amen.

44

A Fair Sense of Humor

By Amy L. Stout

Our mouths were filled with laughter, our tongues with songs of joy. Then it was said among the nations, "The LORD has done great things for them."
~Psalm 126:2

After thirteen years of trying to have a baby the old-fashioned way, and being unsuccessful at achieving our goal, my husband Dan and I decided to pursue adoption.

At one point in the process, we had to meet with the adoption agency's social worker individually. Dan went first, and I waited in the lobby. Our social worker was new to the adoption agency and was still getting accustomed to their forms and way of doing things. As a result, while she was friendly to us, she was also very serious and "all business," concentrating very hard on the task at hand.

Dan sat down at the table across from our social worker, and she proceeded to ask him questions. "How would you describe your complexion?" Never in a million years had Dan expected to be asked that question, and he was quite unprepared to answer. Being caught completely off-guard, he thought for a moment, and then, with the sense of humor my husband was blessed with, replied seriously, "I don't know. Ruggedly handsome?" He flashed a charming smile in her direction.

He thought he would get a laugh or at least a smile in return, but our social worker's face scrunched up, her eyebrows knit together, and a frown formed on her mouth. She looked over the top of her laptop screen. Her eyes studied Dan for a moment, and then she looked back down at her keyboard and said in monotone, "I think we'll go with 'fair.'"

Dan told me later he knew in that moment that: 1) Once I heard about what had happened, he would be no less than dead meat, and 2) our social worker was never going to give us a baby.

Of course, while he was dead meat with me for a time, our social worker did give us a baby, and now we have a wonderful laugh with her about that moment! Turns out, my charming husband made quite the impression on our social worker, and she said she will never forget her "ruggedly handsome" client.

Sometimes, in marriage, you just have to make light of things and laugh your way through them, especially when you are in unfamiliar territory or feel completely out of your element. If we have truly placed our marriage in God's hands, He will write our story so that the ending is always a part of His perfect will. And so that, upon the telling, our story glorifies Him.

My Prayer

Dear God, thank you for giving each of us a unique sense of humor. Help us to value the differences in personality that we have and to realize that, because of you, we are a perfect complement to one another. Use our story to bring honor and glory to you, and help us to laugh along life's journey.

Amen.

Chapter
5

Devotional Stories for Wives

Recapturing the Magic

May the Lord make your love increase and overflow for each other...

~1 Thessalonians 3:12

45

Why I Date My Husband

By Becky Kopitzke

My beloved spoke and said to me, "Arise, my darling, my beautiful one,
come with me..."
~Song of Songs 2:10

She reached for my hand, giggling, eyes wide and sparkling with mischief. "Come on, Mom. We have a surprise for you."

I followed her downstairs. A dusty VCR sat on the basement floor, hooked to our ancient tube television.

"Are you ready?" My husband grinned. Our toddler settled in my lap as her big sister knelt beside us, bursting with excitement. Pop! The black screen sprang to life. I recognized a white satin princess, a raven-haired prince.

Our wedding video.

I thought we had lost it. Through a couple of moves and a cellar flood, that priceless keepsake kept moving until nobody remembered where or when we'd seen it last. In honor of our tenth anniversary, my husband and our four-year-old daughter rummaged through the house until they found the videotape buried in a box. This was my anniversary gift.

Tears ran down my cheeks as I relived the white roses, the vows, and the dress my mother had made.

"Do you like it, Momma?"

"I love it, sweetheart. This is the best surprise ever."

Suddenly, her smile melted to trembling lips, and she sobbed on my shoulder.

"My goodness, what's wrong? Why are you sad?"

"I'm not sad," she choked. "I'm crying because I'm happy!" Seeing her parents together on the video, so blissful and in love, had touched her little heart more than I could have imagined.

That's when I realized—I need to keep dating my husband.

Date night has never been our greatest strength. Excuses are easy when we're busy raising small kids. We're tired; babysitters cost more than dinner; my babies want me to tuck them in… They need me, but not as much as they need two parents united, strong, in love. They need to see Mom fluttery with anticipation of time alone with Dad, to see Dad clasp Mom's fingers while he leads her out the door, blowing kisses to two little girls already immersed in the babysitter's nail polish collection.

They need to know that Mom and Dad are here for them, because we're here for each other first.

It's risky to convince ourselves we're fine without regular dates—without time set aside to rekindle the spark, to remember why we love being together. We can get so absorbed in our daily routines and responsibilities that we forget to make eye contact when we speak. Then we forget to ask what's on each other's mind or what our dreams are. Until we wake up one day wondering what happened to the person we once pursued with all our heart.

When I witnessed our daughter's unfiltered reaction to a video of her parents giddy in love, I caught a glimpse of my marriage through her eyes. And I finally understood. Date night isn't just for my husband and me. Our children need it as much as we do.

My Prayer

*Heavenly Father, thank you for my husband,
my companion. Please help me to set aside
time and attention for him alone so our love
and friendship will grow stronger even during
busy seasons of family life.*

Amen.

46

God Sent Me an E-mail

By Marge Gower

Be devoted to one another in love. Honor one another above yourselves.
~Romans 12:10

Jim and I were devoted to and honored one another through most of our marriage. We got teased unmercifully by some family members, but most of the teasers have gotten divorced. Eventually, though, I got tired of being teased, put my needs before Jim's, and considered it a fair exchange.

Jim and I retired within six months of each other and settled into a new way of life. One morning, I sat absentmindedly deleting e-mails and wondered where our closeness had gone. My heart was overwhelmed with grief. Did anyone understand my agony?

God knew, understood, and sent me an e-mail. I clicked an e-mail containing a devotional, and within the e-mail was an invitation to join a "14-Day Romancing Your Husband Challenge." I was up for His challenge.

Just before Valentine's Day, the first e-mail challenge arrived, containing these four challenges:

Put a chocolate kiss in his briefcase, lunch bag or on the dashboard of his car, with a note that says, "I love you!" (I thought, "He does love his candy. I will put Junior Mints on the table near where he sits to watch TV.")

Write "I love you" on his bathroom mirror with soap or lipstick. (No lipstick, but doable. I will improvise.)

Send a romantic card to his workplace via snail mail. (He's not employed anymore, but I'll put a note by the coffeepot. He usually makes the coffee.)

Draw a candlelight bath and invite him to join you. (Never happened before, and after forty-five years, arthritis, and many more pounds, not happening now. I can light candles in the living room and snuggle close. A cushion usually separates us as I work on my computer.)

God's challenges made me consider other things I had stopped. I didn't surprise Jim with little gifts and cards, put notes in his lunch, bring him coffee in the evening, or make his favorite desserts. I stopped things that nurtured our loving relationship. I waited and waited for Jim to change. What a selfish and lonely way to live.

I've made small changes already, and Jim is responding. I don't ask him for help, but he joins me. Our closeness is returning, and our hearts are healing. My heart and e-mails remain open to God's invitations, as He encourages me.

God reached out to me when my heart was laid open from hurting. I'd still be waiting if He hadn't opened a door through His inviting challenge. A gentle flutter freed my spirit to God's gentle discipline and touched my broken heart.

My Prayer

Dear Lord, help me to find a way to alter my attention from what is missing in my marriage to the rich bounty that is lurking below the surface. May I remember to surrender always to your healing grace. How blessed we are that you work in such mysterious ways.

Amen.

Dad's Away

By Kimberly Porrazzo

"May the LORD keep watch between you and me
when we are away from each other..."
~Genesis 31:49

My husband left us. It's not what you think. A rare business trip took him away for only five days, but during that week of solo parenting, I got a good taste of life as a single mom.

Of course, I thought about him often. The cold and rainy night I had to lug all four of our trashcans to the curb, I was really wishing he was here. When a convention of spiders appeared in our home, I missed him. And whatever it was that was clinking around in my kitchen sink disposal would do so until he got home because there was no way I was reaching into that black hole.

Yes, I missed him. But after twenty years of marriage, I admit I also felt a sense of freedom. For an entire week, I didn't put away any of my curlers, brushes or make-up. I luxuriated in using both the sinks in our master bath and spreading my girl stuff everywhere.

Our queen-size bed—the one I insisted upon early in our marriage because I wanted to "be close"—suddenly felt like the king-size he had always wanted.

And I didn't even think twice about the flannel nightgown.

But the novelty started to wear off after a week of carting both our boys everywhere by myself. I felt it most while checking the locks and turning out the lights before bed.

Apparently, it wasn't just me. As I was helping gather equipment for my younger son's Little League game, he looked at me with a concerned expression and said, "I don't feel like we're going to win today because one of our key people isn't going to be there." He said it with a seriousness that made me listen more closely.

"Who isn't coming?" I asked, trying to guess which of the team's pitchers or best hitters might be absent.

"Dad's not going to be there," he said quietly.

With those words, I was reminded again how important my husband is to this family. "He'll be there in spirit" seemed like an empty promise.

That evening, as I was expecting him to walk in the door, he called. His flight had been canceled due to mechanical problems, and he was to be on another flight that took him through Dallas and on to LAX. He would be home late.

Dozing to the TV while waiting up for him, I was abruptly awakened by a special report of "breaking news." A plane had crashed—something about LAX—and eighteen people were thought to have perished.

Blinking through sleepy eyes, the adrenaline rush kicked in just in time for me to hear the rest of the report. It became clear this was not the plane my husband was on. Relief swept over me as quickly as the panic that had hit me. As I counted my blessings, it occurred to me that this was the plane that carried someone else's husband. And her husband wouldn't be coming home to take out the trash or kill the spiders anymore.

When my husband arrived home at 1:30 A.M., we kissed the quick hello of a tired couple married twenty years and headed upstairs to sleep. As I snuggled up to him and drifted peacefully off to sleep, I smiled, remembering why I wanted that queen-size bed so many years ago.

My Prayer

*Father, I pray that you watch over my
husband as he travels far from our beloved
home. Keep him safe in your protection until
he returns to my loving arms once again.*

Amen.

48

A Harvest of Blessing

By Michelle Shocklee

Even now the one who reaps draws a wage and harvests a crop for eternal life, so that the sower and the reaper may be glad together.
~John 4:36

A s a young bride, I had no idea what older women meant when they said marriage was hard work. "Hard work?" I asked, somewhat surprised. I was blissfully married to my best friend, my college sweetheart. We were having too much fun forging our new life together to consider it work, much less hard. We both had good jobs with comfortable salaries that allowed us to purchase two new vehicles, take weekend trips, and basically enjoy life. A year after our wedding, we bought our first house. Three years later, we brought our first son home, followed two years later by his brother. Life was very full.

That's when the hard work of marriage slapped me in the face.

Consumed with being a good mother, I didn't realize I'd stopped being a good wife. Raising well-adjusted, happy kids became my priority. Because I'd quit my job to stay home with the boys, finances were tight. Stresses we hadn't experienced in our early years of marriage began to chip away at our relationship.

With my husband working long hours, and me filling my days with the boys' school, church and sports activities, plus my own activities and ministries that kept me busy, it was shocking to one day discover how far apart my husband and I had grown. I clearly recall telling a friend that I felt like Brian and I were roommates instead of husband and wife. How had this happened?

Looking back, I see how I let everything and everyone take precedence over Brian and our marriage. I didn't mean to do it nor did I even recognize that it was happening. But after eighteen years of marriage, we'd reached a place where we had to make a decision: Work on our marriage and move forward, or quit.

During those painful months, God made something very clear to me. He'd given me the desire of my heart, which was to be married to my best friend. Brian was my first priority. Being a wife was my most important ministry. I could not continue to put our two precious children ahead of my husband all the time.

With God's help, we made it through those turbulent waters. It took both of us making changes. We had to learn to love and respect each other all over again. This year, we'll celebrate twenty-six years of marriage. And I can honestly say our marriage is healthier and happier than it has ever been. We didn't give up when things got tough, and now we are reaping a harvest of blessing.

My Prayer

*Lord, when things get difficult in my marriage,
may I recall your promise to give us a harvest
if we don't give up. Help me remember
that you first made me a wife, and that my
husband is my priority.*

Amen.

49

From Chaos to Restoration

By Andrea Arthur Owan

*Then Jacob made a vow, saying, "If God will be with me and will
watch over me on this journey I am taking and will give me food to eat
and clothes to wear so that I return safely to my father's household,
then the LORD will be my God..."*
~Genesis 28:20-21

hile studying simplicity, our women's Bible study instructor asked us to determine our individual focus. I laughed outright. Focusing—on anything—was impossible.

In October, my husband, Chris, left a secure job for self-employment, but ensuring the company's success meant grueling work hours, and my younger son and I rarely saw him. He seemed oblivious to the destruction his obsessive behavior wreaked on our marriage and family. Work and success had replaced us, and the rejection felt final. Then my father died, and Christmas was marred by grief. My younger craved his dad's presence; my older son struggled uncharacteristically in college. In April, I battled injuries from a car accident and a hostile insurance company. Finances were shaky, and my marriage hung by a thread. One word summed up my life: chaos.

We'd weathered rough times before in our twenty-seven-year marriage, including our daughter's death, and God had shepherded us through every inch of life's difficulties. Yet now everything seemed to be unraveling. I was at the end of my coping rope, directionless and hopeless.

The one flickering light at the end of the tunnel was our upcoming vacation, but as the departure date neared, the business was at a critical, sink-or-swim juncture. Yet in my mind, this trip had been our last resort, a Hail Mary to save us. What should I do now?

No sooner had I cried out the question than God gave me an answer: go alone. Drive up the California coast? Alone? Having buried my own dreams for so long, I no longer knew my capabilities.

Go alone. It seemed as though God was giving me permission to cease striving and pleasing, to come away with Him. He seemed to say, "Let me take care of you, and everything else." So, I stepped out in faith.

I discarded electronic devices and rejected guilt. I feasted on sunsets, seashores and vistas. I saturated myself with God. I prayed and really listened to Him. As I journeyed, stress dropped like scales from my soul.

And my eyes were opened to how I'd contributed to my marriage's decline. I'd become weak and needy, unfairly expecting Chris to be everything to me. I helped too much, pushed too much, expected too much, enabled too much. I needed to get out of the way and let God work on Chris, so he could grow and become the man he was created to be. As clarity brightened the future, my spirit rejoiced.

Four days before the trip ended, Chris joined me. When I saw him standing curbside at the airport—duffle bag in hand, hopeful, expectant smile on his face—I knew my prayers were answered. Our three-day reunion was honeymoon-like. I shared with Chris everything I'd learned and asked for his forgiveness. Chris apologized for everything he'd done to the family.

Redeemed and restored, our future once again glowed with hope and purpose. I'd trusted God and taken a risk. He'd rewarded us with a miracle.

My Prayer

Thank you, God, for answering when we call, for providing a way out when the road in front of us looks bleak and hopeless or too steep for us to climb. Remind us that often all we need to do is come away with you to listen and rest, and that risks orchestrated by you are worth taking.

Amen.

50

Learning to Be Two Again

By Dawn Byrne

As water reflects the face, so one's life reflects the heart.
~Proverbs 27:19

Our four children had become young adults. Our busy life of running to schools, games and practice, church activities and play dates had wound down. Sitting in front of the TV snuggling with Joe had taken the place of frantic evenings. But without the plethora of responsibilities to coordinate, our conversations dwindled.

One evening after Joe and I arrived home from work, with the kids out, I faced my husband in the middle of our living room, and the stillness of our once lively home struck me. I voiced my anxiety that we might be better together as parents than a couple.

"Joe, do you think we'll get that empty nest syndrome when the kids leave? So many people we know are divorcing. If they can't keep their marriages going after years of trying, maybe it could happen to us."

Joe, standing opposite me in our quiet space, said nothing. But his face burned with angry, wounded feelings, and his body language raged. He stomped upstairs. It was his way of saying, "How can you think that after everything we've been through together?"

I got it. I never hear God's physical voice, but I continue to meditate in His presence and believe in our relationship. Joe and I may not speak much about our relationship, but it is vital in an unexplainable way, even beyond our family.

Alone in the room, I realized our home had become a to-do list instead of a "home." We were a well-oiled machine working singly in the house: I vacuumed, Joe cut the grass; I did laundry and dishes, he did home repairs.

I decided to make a dinner date with Joe. He didn't question the reason for it, but he didn't stand me up either. That was the start of enjoying our empty nester status together.

Today, our three daughters have homes of their own. Our son graduated from high school this year, our thirtieth year of marriage. These almost empty-nest parents woke to the fact that we can still enjoy being a part of fun activities. Only now, we are shuttling ourselves to and from forty-plus hockey practice, eating out, sightseeing and volunteering with Habitat for Humanity. It is still a full life, far from an empty nest.

My Prayer

Dear Father, thank you for your unique
communication that enlightens us in
understanding the unspoken. Help us actively
persist toward harmonious life amidst change.
We praise your powerful awareness that can
come through us.

Amen.

51

What a Difference a Day Makes

By Karen C. Talcott

And let us consider how we may spur one another on toward love and good deeds, not giving up meeting together, as some are in the habit of doing, but encouraging one another...
~Hebrews 10:24-25

The text to my husband read, "Tonight, basketball at 5:30; soccer at 6:30. Which practice are you taking? Dinner will be on the counter." Quick messages here and there represented the majority of our conversations. Life was busy, we were going in different directions, and the family dinner hour was a thing of the past. No longer did we sit around the family table discussing the day's events.

We understood there would be some overlap between interests and sports as our children grew older. But the crazy life we were now leading was solely our fault. We currently had three children on seven sports teams—all at once. Practice was held every night of the week except Tuesdays; games were on both Saturdays and Sundays. The insane schedule was slowly taking a toll on our marriage and family life.

My husband and I grew more distant as the sports season

progressed. We fell into the trap of making our children and their lives the priority. We wanted them to be well rounded and healthy, so besides working hard in school, we encouraged their participation in sports. Yet, as their lives were filled with constant activity, our passion for each other diminished to an all-time low. We made halfhearted attempts to talk each day, but most of our conversations centered on the kids. Date nights were long gone. We had almost-perfect attendance on the soccer field, but not in church.

One night after an evening of running around, my husband and I had a heated argument over nothing in particular. That night, I lay awake thinking about our marriage. It was in a state of disarray, and neither one of us was trying to fix it. In the darkened room, I asked God to help us bridge the gap in our marriage. With all we had done to unravel our vows, could He find a way to bring us closer again?

God's answer came the next morning as I was doing the breakfast dishes. We needed to get away together, even for a short time. We didn't have any family close by, so I did the next best thing I could think of: I called a neighbor. She agreed to take the kids for one day. I reserved a room at a beach hotel for the following weekend. I called my husband, instead of texting him, to tell him about my plan. He was thrilled!

The hotel was two hours from our house, so we talked and talked during the entire car ride. We spent more time talking at the beach and throughout dinner. I had forgotten how much I loved my husband's sense of humor and how good it felt to walk hand in hand on the beach. Sharing a cup of coffee on our patio as the sun rose was one of the most romantic things we had done in years. We returned a mere twenty-four hours after we had left, but what a difference that one day had made in our marriage.

My Prayer

Dear Lord, I ask forgiveness today for filling every nook and cranny of my waking hours with meaningless activities. Help me to simplify my life and remember to spend quiet time with you each day. For it is when we are gentle in spirit that we hear your voice more clearly.

Amen.

52

Kings and Queens

By Nancy B. Gibbs

*Be on your guard; stand firm in the faith; be courageous; be strong. Do
everything in love.*
~1 Corinthians 16:13-14

y husband Roy and I had been married for thirty-
four years before we went on our first cruise
together. Last-minute plans were made, and
together we were sailing off into the deep blue
ocean on a beautiful Sunday afternoon.

During that trip, I realized how we had unintentionally been
allowing our relationship to suffer. Let's just say we took each other
for granted. We didn't argue or bicker. We both simply stayed incredibly busy… too busy for each other.

One night, we decided we would have our breakfast delivered
to our cabin instead of eating in the dining room. The early-morning
meal was not only delicious… it was beautiful. It was fit for a king
and queen. The meal was so pretty that we had a difficult time eating
it.

Finally, we couldn't resist any longer, and by the time we were
done, the plates were a mess. Our napkins were crunched and stained.
They ended up wadded up on the plates, creating quite a mess. Later,
our steward retrieved the dirty plates and cleaned our room.

The next morning, another beautiful meal arrived.

It dawned on me that when people first wed, the marriage is nearly perfect. We admire it. We make our partner feel important and respected. We talk about how beautiful our relationship is, and we are as happy as kings and queens.

But then something happens. We become hungry for our own desires. We allow our own needs to become more important than those of our spouse. Before we know it, our marriages are a mess—much like our plates after breakfast that morning in our cabin. An attempt to draw closer must be made—preferably by both partners.

Going on a cruise is just one way to rekindle the love in marriage. There are many small ways that can add a little spice to our relationships, too. And these actions should take place every day. A little kiss each morning. A hug when we're tired. A heartfelt prayer lifted up at just the right time.

If you want a marriage fit for a king and queen, begin today by adding a little extra time and beauty to your life together.

My Prayer

*Dear God, please help us to remember that
even on days we're not feeling the same kind
of love we felt when we were first wed, love is
still living within our hearts. May we always
look to you for guidance and direction as you
inspire us to treat each other like royalty.*

Amen.

53

Writing on the Wall

By Angela Wolthuis

Let love and faithfulness never leave you; bind them around your neck, write them on the tablet of your heart.
~Proverbs 3:3

Colorful chalk designs on summer sidewalks had always brought a smile to my face, whether I was the artist or the admirer. But I never expected that finding chalk markings on the interior walls of my house as an adult would have the same result, or that I would be the artist!

Between picking up socks and sweeping away dust bunnies from under my sons' beds, I came across a discarded piece of white chalk. The idea came to me in the instant I touched it, and I pursued it before my mom-mind caught up with me. I took to the walls with that chalk and wrote each of my sons a note, listing some of the many things I love about them.

Satisfied with my work, I headed to my own room to pick up socks and clear out the dust bunnies from under my bed. Upon coming up from under the frame, I came face-to-face with the empty space of blue wall above the bed that my husband and I have been blessed to share for thirteen-some years. The words I had written on my sons' walls rolled through my mind, and a question formed in my heart: What words would I have for my spouse? I sat on the edge of the bed for a moment and allowed this thought to linger.

Words have always held great value to me. The very words of the promises and love that God has for me have built up my faith and relationship with Him. I began to think of all these promises and gifts of words that have been written on my walls — the walls of my heart. These words were given at times when I needed to recall that I was loved and cared for unconditionally. As a mother, it took little persuasion to give similar words to my little men, but what about my husband? Did I have words to offer to him? Was I willing to give the gift of words to build and form our relationship? Could I write on his wall?

Ignoring the freshly folded sheets and well-placed pillows, I retrieved the chalk, stood on the bed, and began to write words for my spouse. Even after thirteen years of not-always-wedded-bliss, but of real-life love, I offered the very same gift that is constantly bestowed unto me — words of affirmation and love. As I stepped off the bed, and re-adjusted the sheets and pillows, I smiled.

When my husband came home that day, the boys excitedly showed him their messages. As he entered our room to change after his long day of work, I could almost feel the smile on his face as he took in the message written for him on the wall above our bed. Words don't come easily from me in my marriage, but they are worth all the effort. As God continues daily to write His messages of love and affirmation on the walls of my heart, I can continue to pass on messages of love and affirmation on the walls of my spouse's heart in the hope that our relationship will not only represent the one we can have with our Heavenly Father, but so that it can be built upon the foundation of it.

My Prayer

*Heavenly Father, thank you for the
unconditional love you fill us with; may we
in return be examples of that love to our
husbands. May we build our relationships on
you; give us the grace, the love and the words
to write those affirmations on the tablets of
the hearts of the men you have brought into
our lives as our life partners.*

Amen.

Chapter
6

Devotional
Stories for
Wives

Facing Our Challenges
Together

God is our refuge and strength, an ever-present help in trouble.

~Psalm 46:1

54

For Better or for Worse

By Tammy A. Nischan

For you have been my refuge, a strong tower against the foe. I long to dwell in your tent forever and take refuge in the shelter of your wings.
~Psalm 61:3-4

Taking walks around the campus of the university we attended, my husband-to-be and I often talked of all the things life would hold for us as a married couple. Rainy days were among our favorite times to walk, sharing an umbrella and a sense of closeness in the not-so-pleasant weather. Little did we know just how significant the happy memories of rainy day walks would become as we were called to weather a marriage filled with as many rainy days as sunny ones.

I never dreamed I would watch my husband carry the coffin of our infant daughter Adrienne to a hearse after her death from SIDS in 1992. I never thought that my husband and I would spend more than three years of our marriage traveling back and forth to different oncology offices, surgeries, and chemo treatments with our son who was battling brain cancer, and that this journey with our thirteen-year-old son would end with me listening to my husband speak at Nick's funeral.

When two people decide to live the rest of their lives together "for better or for worse," they usually aren't picturing all of the "for worse" moments that can happen along the way. I know I didn't envision this kind of future as I walked down the aisle to say "I do" to Tim. According to *Jane Brody's Guide to the Great Beyond*, "One-fourth to one-third of parents who lose a child report that their marriage suffers strains that sometimes prove irreparable."

As I reflect on how our marriage has survived such trauma, my mind wanders back to our days of walking under an umbrella together. I believe God planned those moments long ago to teach me a lesson I would not fully grasp until today.

Looking back, I realize that we were able to enjoy those rainy day walks in college because we walked with protection over our heads, we held each other's hand, and we knew that sunny days would follow. Today, in our grief, we share those same figurative truths in our rainy seasons of marriage. God is our shelter overhead in times of storms, we hold onto each other in our sadness, and we know and believe that because God's Son conquered death on the cross, our daughter and son experience a sunny eternity with Him today.

I am thankful today, even though my heart is broken, because the God of rainy days and sunny days leads me and my husband as we walk through this life together... for better or for worse.

My Prayer

Heavenly Father, thank you for being our everlasting source of strength during our trials and tribulations. Even when our hearts are broken, you provide a hope that tomorrow will be better. You are with me and my loved ones, always.

Amen.

On the Path Together

By Carla J. Giomo

The LORD makes firm the steps of the one who delights in him; though he may stumble, he will not fall, for the LORD upholds him with his hand.
~Psalm 37:23-24

One of the challenges of living as a married couple is to learn how to take care of the everyday chores of running a household. Like nearly every bride, I came to our marriage full of optimism, energy, and youthful independence. My husband and I had both lived alone for some time before we married; that, combined with the fact that we are both strong-willed, led us to divide our duties. I took care of some things (cleaning, bookkeeping, laundry and light yard work), and he took care of the rest (cooking, grocery shopping, and cleaning the floors). It worked well for many years, like a relay race where each of us took charge of our own territory.

Our comfortable, efficient lives together came to a screeching halt when my husband had several back-to-back surgeries, and I developed an autoimmune disease that racked me with pain and sapped my energy. Our racing baton had dropped to the ground, and neither of us was able to pick it up.

What did we do? We learned, in fits and starts, to depend upon each other for the most mundane things. When he wasn't allowed to carry things, I did. When I was hurting so badly that all I could do was lie down, he picked up the duster. I became a slightly better cook, and he became more eager to run errands when I was not feeling well. We became less perfectionistic and more compassionate toward each other. It was much like learning how to walk in a three-legged race. What we couldn't do alone we managed to do together.

Walking the three-legged race has put a new shine on our relationship. Our strides may not be as long, but we walk in sync now. We can't get things done as quickly as in the past, but I think we enjoy the trip more. We are more patient with each other, more sympathetic to each other's weaknesses, and more willing to take up the baton when the other falters. It's given birth to a deeper form of partnership.

I am thankful that for nearly twenty years of marriage, we were blessed with good health. But as we face the future, I know that aging and chronic illness will be part of the picture. Perhaps that's how we'll transition to this new phase of our journey: not with efficiency, but with empathy; not with focused minds, but with forgiving hearts; not with compulsive doing, but with compassionate being. And we'll walk that path together, strides matching, with his arm around my shoulders and my hand on his side.

My Prayer

May I listen this day more to the condition of our souls and bodies, and less to the demanding voice of my to-do list. May I be open to giving help when it is needed and to receiving help when I am in need. May I match my stride to the steps of the one I love as we travel our life's path together.

Amen.

56

Trail to Tenderness

By Kim Harms

Your eyes will see the king in his beauty and view a land that stretches afar.
~Isaiah 33:17

It was raining when we reached the trailhead. Everything in me wanted to beg Corey to turn around and take me to a hotel. But I kept quiet, pulled a poncho over my head and got in step behind my husband on the Superior Hiking Trail. I struggled with my attitude all through the wet, muddy night, wondering why in the world I had ever agreed to such a trip.

"How are you holding up?" Corey asked, as we lay side-by-side in our sleeping bags.

I wanted to scream, "How am I holding up? Are you serious? I am miserable!" But instead I replied with a curt "surviving" as I rolled over to go to sleep.

I married a man who loves adventure, and for the first several years of our lives together, he was happy to go on his wilderness explorations without me. But when he requested I don a backpack and hike a portion of the Superior Trail with him, I knew I had to say yes even though I didn't want to. You see, a backpacking trip with my husband meant no running water and no toilets. It meant filtering drinking water from streams, fending off mosquitoes all day and sleeping in a tiny tent on the hard ground. Basically, it was the opposite of what I consider a relaxing getaway. But I love my husband, and I knew he wanted me to take part in his passion for the outdoors, so I agreed, albeit begrudgingly.

After a rainy first night, we awoke to sunshine, and God reminded me that love as He commands it is not just a warm fuzzy feeling, but a choice followed by action. So, on day two, I chose to love my husband by focusing on the good instead of the bad. That choice led to a gradual change in my attitude. I found that I enjoyed walking steps behind Corey through thick forests of trees without another soul around. I felt a sense of accomplishment when we reached the peak of Mount Trudee, and I was filled with awe when we stopped at an overlook with a view of the vast expanse of Lake Superior. When I finally quit feeling sorry for myself, I recognized what a gift it was to see Corey in all his rugged outdoor splendor. And I realized that eating a rice dinner out of a baggie on a tree stump beside my husband is actually pretty romantic.

Not only did I discover that I enjoy backpacking, but my decision to love Corey by taking part in his passion actually drew us closer together as a couple. I felt a deep tender connection to him by experiencing his enthusiasm for the outdoors, and he felt loved in a new way, knowing that I had stepped a million miles out of my comfort zone for his sake.

My Prayer

*Dear God, please help me to recognize
opportunities to show my husband I love
him through my actions. Bless me with the
foresight to look beyond my own desires and
the courage to step out of my comfort zone
to show the man I'm committed to just how
much I love him.*

Amen.

"Dinner's ready, honey, would you like it with or without mosquitoes?"

Reprinted by permission of
Stephanie Piro ©2013

57

Quiet in the Midst of Chaos

By Michelle Crystal

*"Ask and it will be given to you; seek and you will find;
knock and the door will be opened to you."*
~Matthew 7:7

Scott's face was as pale as the sheet that was stretched across his chest. The white mound moved up and down with his breath—I watched to make sure. His eyes were large, light blue frightened circles that were searching mine for comfort. I latched onto his hand and squeezed; it was slippery with sweat and unnaturally cold. Bending down to feel his hands against my face, I reveled in his familiar scent and kissed his lips; they were so cold, it chilled me deep down. Tears fell as he spoke. "I'm sorry."

Fear stole my breath, but I managed to say "I love you" as they wheeled him away.

I stood there with my hand trembling in mid-air, staring past the blurry double doors that swung closed, too stunned to move. It had all happened too quickly to fully register in my brain. Severe chest pain; a lightning fast drive to the ER; a flurry of gloved hands and wires hooked to every inch of his body; doctors rattling off questions while

I fumbled for answers; and alarms I barely heard over the pounding of my own heart. I just remember staring at my husband's face and thinking he looked as lifeless as his mother did when I dressed her frozen body for the funeral. This couldn't be happening.

I wandered into the waiting room, alone, more scared than I knew possible, and sat down heavily, barely breathing. The television hummed with action, and an intercom system called out muffled names as the elevator dinged repeatedly. The smell of stale coffee and the weight of grief turned my stomach sour. I was twenty-nine years old and happily married for eleven years, with four small children at home. How does a woman who's not yet thirty face the possibility of becoming a widow? Dear God, I thought, are you even there?

Pulling out my cell phone, I called my mother and sobbed until I couldn't breathe. When I hung up, I didn't feel any better. In fact, panic and doubt had made me hysterical. Pacing the small room like a caged beast, my heart rammed up against my ribcage, and my breath came out in several short bursts. It was late. I didn't want to disturb my friends, my mom and dad lived hundreds of miles away, and my sister was watching my children, but I desperately needed relief. Where could I turn for peace? In my heart, I knew the answer, but I lacked the courage to try.

Knock and the door will be opened to you. I stumbled out into the hallway, where the bright fluorescent lights assaulted my swollen eyes, and searched for a quiet place. Dropping to my knees, I called out to God, pushing aside my fear and relying on a fleeting flicker of faith. In the wee hours of night, I turned my heart to the Father—and He gave me, as promised, His peace.

My husband survived. I will be forever grateful for that priceless gift, and also for His wordless message: In a life of chaos and uncertainty, we must fall to our knees to find the strength to stand.

My Prayer

Lord, what a gift it is that you stay with us in our intense trials and never let us go. Even when I am full of uncertainty, your divine presence comforts my soul and brings me peace.

Amen.

Balancing the Scales

By Deborah Sturgill

Surely your goodness and love will follow me all the days of my life,
and I will dwell in the house of the LORD forever.
~Psalm 23:6

At age thirty-two, I met Detective Mike—a tall, dark, handsome, Christian man with a hilarious sense of humor. We dated two years, got married and affectionately nicknamed each other "Bo." We had a fairytale wedding at a flower-covered chalet, surrounded by family and friends.

The fairy tale eventually turned into everyday life. Mortality rates for police officers are very high—and I was starting to see why. The good-natured man who left the house in the mornings often returned home with a clenched jaw and a cynical mood. Some days, it seemed like a black storm cloud loomed over his head. He loved his job, but I knew my funny Bo was exposed to dark forces every day.

One summer, we decided to get away to the beach. A few days into the trip, I noticed the happy-go-lucky man I married re-emerge—joking with strangers and laughing out loud.

"This is awesome... the ocean air, the sunshine, the friendly people. I feel like a new man. I wish it was vacation every day!" he said.

Then I realized that if Bo was going to handle the stress of being a police officer, and live long enough to enjoy a happy retirement, he absolutely needed a vacation every single day.

Since that day, I try to bring as much bright light into Mike's week as possible by packing him delicious homemade veggie soups for lunch, letting him watch unlimited "guy shows" on television, encouraging him to go fishing with his best friend Jim, and listening to inspirational speakers with our morning coffee, to name a few. My goal is to help balance the scales between light and darkness in my officer's life. As Milton Berle once said, "Laughter is an instant vacation!"

My Prayer

*Dear Lord, I pray today for the husbands
who willingly serve and protect us in
dangerous jobs. Surround them with angels
to protect their minds, bodies, and spirits. Let
their days be full of goodness and light.*

Amen.

59

A Spirit of Thanksgiving

By Sandy Knudsen

Give thanks in all circumstances; for this is God's will for you in Christ Jesus.
~1 Thessalonians 5:18

W hen I signed up to be Ray's helpmate "till death do us part," I never realized the depth of this commitment. My role became not only that of a wife, but as caregiver for more than twenty years.

Our journey together began July 17, 1982. Like any newly married couple, we had many dreams and aspirations. We had been married only four years when Ray was diagnosed with a rare form of degeneration of the cerebellum. In plain English, every motor area would be affected, and complete disability was inevitable.

By 1995, Ray was dependent upon me for almost everything. He needed my assistance for dressing, personal hygiene, and feeding. Caring for two young children, working as a part-time teacher, and caring for Ray filled almost every waking moment.

Although Ray's body was being ravaged by disability, his spirit continued to soar. His love and faith in God never waned. He had a real zest for life and always seemed to be thankful.

Ray and I both knew we still had plenty to be thankful for. By the grace of God, his mind stayed alert. He stayed engaged in life even though he lost most of his ability to communicate orally and experienced some hearing loss.

Despite all of his disabilities, Ray remained a positive teacher. He taught me so much about faith and trust—simply learning to take God at His Word.

I learned many lessons on this journey, but a primary one was the importance of cultivating a thankful spirit. No matter how negative our circumstances looked, we knew there was always something to be thankful for.

Many days were very hard and the struggles intense, but Ray was still with me, and he was a wonderful companion. His positive attitude was such a strength and encouragement to me. Ray possessed an uncanny sense of humor, which helped in keeping the stress level down.

I am eternally grateful that Ray was in my life for twenty-six years. His love, joy, and encouragement are still very much a part of my life today.

If you look closely, you will see there is always something to be thankful for. I believe the more you can cultivate a spirit of thanksgiving, the more your eyes are open to the beauty and the gifts in your life. So far, my life's journey has seen its share of hardship and pain. But through all of the difficulties, I believe that I have become stronger. I continue to see the beauty, love and faithfulness of God shine through, and I am thankful.

My Prayer

*Heavenly Father, when the circumstances of
life are getting me down, may you remind
me that I have so much to be thankful for.
Life can be hard, but I can still choose to be
thankful. Open my eyes, Lord, so I can see
the beauty around me.*

Amen.

60

Two Are Better than One

By Amy Sayers

Two are better than one, because they have a good return for their labor.
~Ecclesiastes 4:9

I had gone almost twenty-seven years without a seizure, so when I began having them again at the age of forty-five, it really turned my world upside-down. When the doctor told me I couldn't drive for six months, my heart just sank. I don't live in the town where I teach, and my husband David would have to rearrange his daily schedule to accommodate getting me to work on time. And that was only part of it. What about meetings, running quick errands, or a day of shopping? My independence quickly turned to total dependence on friends and, most often, David.

But it didn't take long for me to see that my husband had the hands and feet of Jesus. David would play games on his phone or read a book while he waited for me to finish lesson plans or shop, and he never once complained. When I climbed into the vehicle, I was always greeted the same way—with a smile, a kiss, and a "How was your day?" It didn't matter if he had waited two minutes or two hours!

On the last morning that David had to take me to work, neither of us was prepared for the tears or feelings of sweet sadness we would feel. We had become accustomed to taking that driving time together to talk about our day and things that were troubling us, or to share our hopes and dreams. God had used what we thought would be an inconvenience to draw us closer together and help us to see just how strong our love is.

Over the years, we have experienced a lot in our marriage. Each year's joys and concerns knit our hearts closer together, but it wasn't until my epilepsy decided to rear its ugly head that we truly learned about giving and receiving unconditional love. I learned that when your spouse, like Jesus, holds out his hand to you, you accept it with love and thankfulness, and let him pull you up. It's God's way of bringing two hearts closer together.

My Prayer

*Father, thank you for giving me a helpmate
who not only shares in my hopes and dreams,
but encourages me when life is hard. Thank
you for using the difficult times in our lives to
knit our hearts together, and always remind
me to show him my appreciation in loving
ways.*

Amen.

We Will Trust God

By Sue Tornai

I lift up my eyes to the mountains — where does my help come from?
My help comes from the LORD, the Maker of heaven and earth.
~Psalm 121:1-2

Wrapped in each other's arms, we wept in a crowded pharmacy. John and I had been together through his major surgeries — prostate cancer, bleeding colon, hernia and broken ankle. But now, after nineteen years, his cancer was back. We met with the oncologist, and he prescribed the latest, greatest cancer-fighting drug. When the pharmacy clerk quoted the price for one month, we thought there must be a mistake. She checked. There was no mistake. John and I looked at each other.

"But what if the medicine makes John sick after the first pill? What if it doesn't work?" I asked, and received a blank look.

"Do you have a sample size prescription?" I asked.

"This is what your doctor prescribed," she said.

We went back to the doctor's office, and he prescribed a smaller amount. When we returned to the pharmacy, we discovered it would be more cost-efficient to buy the full amount for a month. The bill was $1,956.77.

We walked together to the parking lot.

"I'm not worth it," John said.

Tears filled my eyes. I remembered a time in my life when I had said, "I'm not worth it," thinking God's forgiveness couldn't possibly cover all my sin. I was wrong, and so was John. God showed me how much He loved me, and He became a faithful friend.

"We will trust God," I said. "Let's watch and see what He does." I don't know where the words came from, but I knew this was God's opportunity. Who else could we turn to?

So far, the medication has not been effective against the cancer, but thankfully John is not in pain. He maintains his sense of humor and keeps busy with his projects in the garage. He lives every day as if it's his last. Each day with him is sweeter than the day before.

Although we have not traveled this road before, we are clinging to our faith to get us through. "I lift up my eyes to the mountains—where does my help come from? My help comes from the LORD, the Maker of heaven and earth" (Psalm 121:1-2).

My Prayer

Father God, you have led us through tough times in our marriage. We trust you now, knowing you are always with us. Thank you for your mercy and strength. We pray for healing and recovery.

Amen.

Stand by Me

By Jayne Thurber-Smith

Although the Lord gives you the bread of adversity and the water of afflic-tion, your teachers will be hidden no more; with your own eyes you will see them. Whether you turn to the right or to the left, your ears will hear a voice behind you, saying, "This is the way; walk in it."
~Isaiah 30:20-21

Eight years ago, my husband Peter was given an awesome career opportunity that required us to relocate our family of six a distance of 600 miles. The stress of moving and adjusting to a new community, four unhappy kids, and long hours at Peter's new job all took a severe toll on our seventeen-year marriage. Within a few months, we were stretched to the breaking point.

My wonderful sister-in-law and I are e-mail pen pals, and she was my lifeline through it all. Although I didn't go into details about my marital problems with her, she sensed a cry for help and finally wrote, "Sometimes we all need a little assistance. A few years ago, your brother and I were in the exact same spot. If we hadn't gone to a marriage seminar, I don't think we would have gotten through it."

I was shocked. They had always had the perfect marriage; everyone knew it. To me, marriage counseling was for those who didn't have a good relationship. She was real enough to let me know they had needed help and got it. I realized there was nothing wrong with that. I had been married long enough to know that staying married took hard work, but now I was realizing that sometimes you need an unbiased party to help you work through it all.

Peter and I met with our pastor, and he really did help us see things much more clearly, like a lighthouse beam breaking through a fog. Everything he said was common sense, but when you're going through difficult, emotional transitions, you're not thinking sensibly. He helped us realize that instead of thinking of each other as the enemy, we needed to draw on each other's strength through these trials, lean on each other and the Lord, and emerge victorious. We needed to decide that defeat was not an option.

Now I know there's no such thing as a perfect marriage, but those striving to get there can get just a little closer when they're not afraid to ask for help. It makes perfect sense.

My Prayer

Dear Heavenly Father, we ask you to please lead us, bless us and continue to bind us together with cords that cannot be broken. We thank you for your teachers, who help us along the way. May we never hesitate to cry for help when we need it.

Amen.

Chapter 7

Devotional Stories for Wives

Surrender It All

Do not conform to the pattern of this world, but be transformed by the renewing of your mind. Then you will be able to test and approve what God's will is—his good, pleasing and perfect will.

~Romans 12:2

Employed by God

By Krisan Murphy

...be content with what you have, because God has said, "Never will I leave you; never will I forsake you."
~Hebrews 13:5

After years of full-time Christian ministry, twenty years of marriage, and four children, my husband, Mike, was suddenly jobless. I reasoned that with his excellent education and work experience, a job would be easy to find. I was wrong.

After he searched unsuccessfully for weeks, my diligent husband worked a variety of labor jobs, from washing windows to cleaning roofs. I prayed that the Lord would give him a "real" job, and I began teaching at the small Christian school our children attended.

A year passed, and I imagined that the Lord had made a mistake. Surely, He didn't want this lifestyle for us, which seemed unbearable at times. But another year passed — and then two, three, four, and five. After six years, Mike had regular repeat customers who needed his handyman and construction services. Still, I searched the want ads often for a professional job for Mike. Nothing materialized.

The newspaper constantly had want ads for nurses, so I hinted and eventually pleaded with Mike to consider going back to school for nursing. After all, I reasoned, how long could he climb ladders and swing a hammer? My energy was drained, too, from the challenges of teaching, rearing teenage boys and twin daughters.

But one evening when I heard the familiar noise of Mike's truck pulling into the driveway after dark, I wondered what kind of wife I had been to my hard-working husband. Had I been nagging him for years about getting a better job? Had I been disgruntled about how he had provided for us?

While the children were in bed that night, with my school papers spread out over the table for grading, I bowed my head and prayed, "Forgive me, Lord! I've been ungrateful. Thank you for the ways in which you have provided for our family through my husband."

When Mike walked through the door the next evening, I hugged him and thanked him for his hard work. I told him that I would no longer say that he was "looking for a real job." He worked diligently and provided. And if that was the work the Lord had for him, then I was thankful.

Surrendering my will to the Lord gave me a deep peace, and also resulted in an unexpected surprise. When I stepped aside, close college friends of Mike encouraged and counseled him in a renewed effort to search for a professional job. Seven years after my husband lost his job, and only weeks after I gave up my will, the Lord provided for Mike to make the impossible leap into a job in the engineering field—even though he had not worked in that profession for more than twenty-five years. When I finally learned the lesson the Lord wanted to teach me, He provided in an extraordinary way.

My Prayer

Dear Lord, open my eyes to ways I am ungrateful to my husband for his provision. Give me courage and faith to be continually thankful instead of discontented, and to trust you to provide when I cannot see how you will do it.

Amen.

64

The Compromise

By Carol Emmons Hartsoe

The LORD gives strength to his people;
the LORD blesses his people with peace.
~Psalm 29:11

uring the early years of our marriage, my husband and I often disagreed about money. Our priorities were worlds apart, and sometimes it seemed that we would never come to an agreement. Although our combined salaries were enough to get by, we never seemed to have enough money for extras, like making improvements to the fixer-upper home we lived in.

One year, we were excited to learn we would receive a sizable tax refund... and then the debate began. My husband wanted to build a large shed in the back yard to hold the lawn mower, tools and other things that cluttered our garage. As for me, I dreamed of having a nice front porch with rails all around and a swing. I imagined many hours of relaxation and enjoyment for us, our families, and our friends. It was a matter of need versus want. We had many discussions.

Each of our discussions began nicely enough. We calmly shared our ideas and stated the pros and cons for each. Still, our "discussions" repeatedly turned into heated arguments with no apparent solutions.

One Sunday morning while attending church services, I realized suddenly that I had not prayed about this problem. This tax refund was such a blessing to my family, and I had not even been thankful for it. I had been so busy trying to justify my reasons for wanting a porch, and arguing with my husband, that I had neglected to ask God for guidance.

That morning, I gave the problem to the Lord and prayed that peace would be restored to my home. I asked that I would be strong enough to accept the outcome of this dilemma, even if it did not go my way.

A few months later, we began building a shed out in our back yard. Yes, my husband got his shed. I was at peace with that, especially when he began adding a porch to it, complete with rails and a swing.

My "front" porch was actually in the back yard, although it turned out to be the perfect spot. It was near the garden and was a shady place to rest and enjoy a cool drink with my girls on hot summer days. I often sat in the swing watching them play as I shelled beans and peas. Many evenings, we also shared this spot with our neighbors as we chatted and supervised our children while they spent time together.

My husband and I have now been married almost forty years. We often think back to those earlier days and remember the joy our family has experienced, thanks to making a simple compromise. Of course, we had a little help!

My Prayer

Dear Heavenly Father, thank you for the many blessings you send our way. We are grateful, Lord, for strength and peace… and for the joy we find if only we will come to you.

Amen.

65

A Warm Embrace

By Deanna Broome

If I rise on the wings of the dawn, if I settle on the far side of the sea, even there your hand will guide me, your right hand will hold me fast.
~Psalm 139:9-10

The house was quiet, too quiet. I shut the door behind me and walked upstairs. With every step, I felt heavier, sadder, and more alone. The long-awaited deployment was here, and the countdown began today. Two hundred and ten days without my husband. I felt the full weight of being both Mom and Dad on my shoulders. I knew my middle-school twin sons needed me to be strong, but inside I was ready to crumble. I decided that the tears would have to come later. For now, I had the morning school routine to focus on.

Waking the boys, I felt so sad for them. They had said goodbye to their dad the night before. It was always difficult to watch those last hugs and pep talk from Joe. They were older now with this deployment, and he reminded them to "help Mom out." Both Connor and Hunter masked their sadness and told him, "Yes, sir." I knew their hearts were hurting as much as mine. As they woke up and silently dressed, I tried to keep the conversation light. I made breakfast and put on Christian music, which always lifted my spirit. I choked back my tears. My sons gathered their backpacks and headed out the door.

Somehow, I just knew those backpacks were a lot lighter than the burden they bore in their sad hearts.

Standing in my kitchen, the tears came and wouldn't stop. I felt so incredibly lonely and needed a hug from my husband. Suddenly, I heard a tender voice deep in my soul. The Lord told me, "Deanna, put your arms around yourself right now." I took my arms and wrapped them around me. Then His voice came again: "This is what I am doing while Joe is away. I am holding you." At that moment, I knew Jesus was right there with me, embracing a brokenhearted woman. The sadness left me, and I never felt so loved. I clung to His warm embrace over and over again throughout the deployment. It made me stronger and beautifully connected to the One and Only who gives us peace.

Hugs mean something different to me now. When my husband is away for long durations, I know Jesus is ready to wrap me in His arms. He also taught me to never take for granted the hug of my precious husband because he is a gift showing how much God loves me.

My Prayer

*My loving Father, thank you for your
unfailing love and faithfulness in my
life. Hold me today and fill me with your
unsurpassed peace. I surrender any feelings
of loneliness because I know you are always
with me.*

Amen.

I Surrender

By Linda Kosinski Maynard

A gentle answer turns away wrath, but a harsh word stirs up anger.
~Proverbs 15:1

We had hit another impasse in our communication. My husband, Marcel, thought he was right, but I knew I was. It's exhausting going over the same ground repeatedly, unable to come to a compromise. I retreated to the bedroom. I said I needed time to think, but I really wanted to sulk.

I am a right-brained thinker. That goes with my creative abilities and artistic bent. Marcel, on the other hand, is left-brained. He sees things in set patterns. Spreadsheets excite him. I've been told more than once, by my black-and-white thinker, that I am too wishy-washy and people take advantage of me. I like the color grey, though. So here we were, years into our marriage, still plowing through familiar rocky ground.

I knew I was partly to blame. My pride made it hard to apologize, but I knew I needed to do just that. Would I rather be "right" or unified?

A clever idea came to me. My heart leapt. For a creative person, ideas are gold.

I got a wire hanger and took it apart. Once I had straightened it, I bent it into a slight arc, kind of like a fishing pole. I got one of Marcel's white hankies and tied it to one end.

Slipping into the living room where he was sitting, I poised the hanger over his head and dipped it until the hankie was at his eye level. He jumped, and I yelled, "I surrender!"

The air that had been so thick minutes before cleared up. We really laughed.

After that day, surrender became a tradition with us. Whenever we would get into similar spots, one of us would grab a hankie or a tissue and fling it at the other. It worked to defuse the tension every time.

One day, I was rushing to go out of town. We argued. Being behind schedule, I didn't kiss him good-bye. I had never done that before. My stomach tightened later as I approached home. On our flagpole was one of Marcel's white T-shirts, waving in all its glory.

At my son and daughter-in-law's Jack and Jill Shower, I told the story of our surrendering tradition. I took out a beautifully wrapped cylindrical package. Inside were a dozen men's handkerchiefs tied together. I removed them one by one, saying, "These represent the instances in which you can decide: Would you rather be right—or would you rather be unified?"

Trust me, having to be right is just not worth it.

My Prayer

Lord, sometimes, in the most important relationships in our life, we can be the most obstinate. We can be stingy with grace in our homes. Teach me to forgive with my whole heart and love the differences in my spouse. When I am humble, I am most like you.

Amen.

Reprinted by permission of
Stephanie Piro ©2013

67

True Home

By Jennifer Cardine

Better to live on a corner of the roof than share a house
with a quarrelsome wife.
~Proverbs 25:24

I had worked my way through college and settled into the life I imagined for myself by my mid-twenties: a happy marriage, a decent job and a new baby. Then my husband and I decided to invest in real estate and bought a small house with an affordable mortgage payment. Our little family moved into the house, and then I got pregnant again just as the economy crashed. Suddenly, our mortgage was bigger than our home's newly diminished value, and our family was bigger than our home. We were stuck in a house that we did not want and could not afford to leave.

As I drove our toddlers to a play date, I was feeling sorry for myself. I lowered the radio volume, sighed and reached out to God. "I don't know what to do, God. I don't know how to be content in our house. I don't know how to be thankful. Please help me."

I looked at my wedding rings, glimmering in the sunlight as my fingers wrapped around the steering wheel. They contained a sapphire my future husband had slipped on my finger with a smile and a question, and a line of diamonds he used to promise forever. I thought about my parade of blessings: the sacrifices my husband had made so I could spend my days with our children; how little he complained and how cool he was when I did; the great love he had for me and how that love nurtured us through a three-year long-distance relationship; the exhale at the end of the day when he entered the house and helped carry the burden; the last bite of a shared dessert he always left for me.

I could only offer God a knowing smile when I recalled Proverbs 25:24: "Better to live on a corner of the roof than share a house with a quarrelsome wife." I knew what my heart wanted—no, craved—and it was not a lovely home. I had what money could not buy. The economy might have been crashing but my relationship was booming.

My Prayer

*God, please help me to continually recognize
the great blessings you have given my
husband and me. I want to focus on the
priceless gift you have given me in this man
and live my life in gratitude.*

Amen.

68

Lord, Use Me

By Barbara Alpert

But a married man is concerned about the affairs of this world—how he can please his wife—and his interests are divided. An unmarried woman or virgin is concerned about the Lord's affairs: Her aim is to be devoted to the Lord in both body and spirit. But a married woman is concerned about the affairs of this world—how she can please her husband.
~1 Corinthians 7:33-34

Have you ever asked God to use you in a new and greater way? Several months ago, I did, but God's response was not what I imagined. I thought He would widen my ministry at the nursing home, possibly have me lead a women's small group or increase my availability to mentor a close friend.

Shortly after my "Lord, Use Me" request, my husband needed leg surgery. At first, I did pretty well managing the added duties, but as time evolved, so did unexpected further demands. For months, my husband was unable to walk, drive, go anywhere, or do much on his own. Overnight, God turned me into a full-time nurse, chauffeur, waiter, and even a landscaper on top of my normal routine and outside obligations. Through this upheaval, God taught me a valuable life lesson: Marriage, family, and home life are a ministry.

Trouble came when I tried to hang onto my outside ministries while God was summoning me to at-home ministry. Although I professed, "I can do all this through him who gives me strength" (Philippians 4:13), I did not learn the priceless lesson God was teaching until everything became unbearable. God was giving me all the strength I needed to minister, aid, and support my husband through his lengthy recovery and keep our home in order, but I had to learn the hard way. As I learned to pull back from the other obligations to tend to my husband's extra needs, my load became light, manageable, and even enjoyable. Months later, my husband recovered, and the other stuff was still there to do.

If you are married, your ministry is toward your spouse. If you have children, your ministry is toward them, too. God loves a servant's heart, but if He has blessed you with a family, then you are responsible to take good care of what He has entrusted to your care. Priorities need to start in the home—and then spread to careers, important friendships, and ministerial pursuits. Refuse to allow too many outside obligations to steal your vital role as a spouse and parent. Make a commitment within your home to serve, respect and value one another, as God would have it. As written in Ecclesiastes 4:12, "Though one may be overpowered, two can defend themselves. A cord of three strands is not quickly broken." Allow God to be the third strand that binds your family together. Then other ministry pursuits will prosper.

My Prayer

*Heavenly Father, pardon me if I have erred
as a godly servant to my spouse or family.
Reveal to me what things may have to go so
nothing can separate my love and obligation
to my loved ones. Teach me your ways so I
can be all that you would have me to be for
my loved ones.*

Amen.

69

In Due Season

By Pamela Jarmon-Wade

And let us not grow weary while doing good,
for in due season we shall reap if we do not lose heart.
~Galatians 6:9 (NKJV)

There was a time when my husband did not go to church with me. I would go alone and long for my husband to be by my side. I would get so angry when he did not have a valid reason for not going. I knew for a fact that he believed in the same God as me. We had both grown up in the Baptist church. I even took a hiatus from church to see if that would make a difference, but it did not.

After returning home from church on Sunday evenings, I would be unloving, critical, disappointed, and unforgiving toward my husband. Then one day, the words from a sermon stuck with me: "Love him more and keep praying."

From that day forward, I changed my reaction to his Sunday rebuttals. I not only kept praying for my husband to change, but I also began praying for me to change. I prayed for God to help me love my husband unconditionally, and to make my prayers a true language of love. I asked Him to show me how to be more patient, more loving and forgiving, and less critical.

In the meantime, I continued to invite my husband to attend

church with no expectations. I accepted his "not this Sunday" replies with love and kindness, cheerfully shared my sermon notes, and showed no signs of disappointment. I would interact with a new-found acceptance that I should not grow weary for wanting what would be pleasing to God.

One Sunday, he got up and started getting ready for church before I could ask. He has been going ever since. If, for some reason, I do not attend, he will go without me and purchase the CD at the church bookstore for me. I was never that thoughtful.

I praise God for answering prayers, making us a team, and allowing me to learn how to overlook faults or weaknesses for the greater good of my marriage. My husband's spiritual growth was not at the same pace as mine, but "in due season" we came together in Christ's love.

My Prayer

Lord, when I seek to change my husband's ways, please remind me that perhaps the change needs to begin with me. Help me to show forgiveness and love when he disappoints me, and to allow our lives to unfold according to your perfect timing.

Amen.

70

Socks

By Lynn Dove

...to be made new in the attitude of your minds...
~Ephesians 4:23

My husband has this strange habit. He calls it logical organization. I used to call it annoying, but I have put up with it for nearly thirty-five years, so now it is almost endearing. Yeah, I said it... what was once annoying is now endearing. How did that happen? Explanation: being married for close to thirty-five years!

Charles has a little sock pile on the floor on his side of our bed. Usually, there are at least three pairs of socks in it. One pair is his dress socks. Another is a pair of white tube socks he wears with his jeans. The last pair are usually soiled and holey but, as he says, "good enough to work on cars with." He has this system of "recycling" through his socks during any given week. Since he only uses his dress socks for work, he can usually get two days' wear out of them. His casual tube socks he can sometimes stretch to three wearable days, and his "working-on-car socks" are worn until they nearly fall off his feet. It is a system he has had since we got married. Try as I might to pick up the socks and organize them in my own way by throwing them in the laundry, or at least putting them in a drawer so I don't have socks on the floor, Charles prefers his method.

Today, as I made the bed and stepped over his little pile of socks, I wanted to act annoyed. Instead, I laughed out loud and then picked up one of the tube socks and lovingly held it in my hand.

A dear friend of ours lost her sweet husband a while ago. Theirs was a marriage that all of us dream of having. Laughing side-by-side, hand-in-hand, raising children together and loving their grandchildren, they were indeed the "perfect" couple. She sits alone in church now. Yes, she is surrounded by her friends and family, but her best friend is no longer by her side. She used to complain once in a while to me about some of her husband's quirky habits, but now she just smiles in remembrance of him.

I can't imagine life without my best friend by my side.

I look at the sock in my hand, and then look down to see a week's worth of his "sock organization." Annoying, yes, but as I drop the tube sock back onto the pile, I praise God for my husband.

I can't imagine what it would be like if I never again saw his socks there on the floor beside the bed.

My Prayer

*Lord, thank you for my husband, and
especially for all his endearing quirks and
habits. I praise you for the years we have had
together. I humbly pray that you might give
me many, many more years married to my
best friend.*

Amen.

Reprinted by permission of
Stephanie Piro ©2013

71

Quit to Win

By Amber Rose Cavalier

*Do not be anxious about anything, but in every situation, by prayer
and petition, with thanksgiving, present your requests to God.
And the peace of God, which transcends all understanding,
will guard your hearts and your minds in Christ Jesus.*
~Philippians 4:6-7

"Ha! You'll quit smoking the day I get pregnant!" I snapped, immediately rueful of my sharp tone. My husband, a nicotine poster child since the ripe age of fifteen, remained silent. It wasn't my first outburst about his ugly, health-destructive habit, but it was one that signaled my losing battle with faith in our war of infertility.

We had been married for three years, blessed in sacramental bliss by our parish priest. For some couples, three years would seem barely a moment in time. But for Chuck and me, three years had ushered him into middle age and set my maternal clock into overdrive.

Everything from reading social media to walking through a grocery store left me feeling that the entire female population, teenage and pre-menopausal alike, seemed to be reproducing at rabbit pace, without any difficulty whatsoever. I had to walk away when a coworker whined about morning sickness, and Chuck found himself biting his tongue when his teenage students, late in pregnancy, waddled across campus, sans wedding bands, jobs and, often, transportation. We found ourselves envious and frustrated when Chuck's middle-aged sister announced a surprise pregnancy to add to her household of three teenagers. It seemed as if the world was mocking our prayers. I was beginning to lose faith that we would have the child we so desperately wanted.

During one especially difficult week, Chuck expressed his desire to quit smoking after nearly thirty years, and my pessimism got the best of me. Tears filled my eyes, and I walked away. I was disgusted by my lack of patience and faith. That night, I offered one more heartfelt prayer to God—for happiness in our marriage covenant. I would stop praying for a pregnancy that I felt might never happen. I would toss the charts, thermometer, and calendars that had taken over our bedroom. I would not bicker with my lover as a result of our infertility frustrations. I left it all in God's hands. After all, why would I want to bring an innocent child into an unhappy relationship that lacked trust in God?

Two weeks later, Chuck was invited to attend a conference in Las Vegas, and I joined him. A weekend business trip had turned into a much-anticipated vacation. As I mentally checked off our packing list, including his usual box of Marlboros, he teased, "Are you sure you want to take up smoking? I quit seven days ago."

I was floored. I had been so wrapped up in my own despair that I had failed to see my husband's success. Elated, we threw ourselves into an exciting and memorable trip. I attributed my late period to the stress of flying.

Upon arriving home, Chuck asked when my cycle was due. Ironically, he had never asked before, and I stammered my surprised reply, "Five days ago."

I hauled out an old pregnancy test, and three minutes later it showed the faintest of two pink lines. I didn't need to dig the fertility calendar out of the wastebasket to know that God had blessed us with a child on the very night of my cynical outburst.

Years have passed, and I am reminded daily of God's love and His plan. Chuck is still smoke-free, and our beautiful son, Johnathon, recently started preschool. He is such a blessing, and I can never thank my Lord enough for sharing him with us.

My Prayer

*Lord, help me to trust in you when the desires
of my heart seem to go unanswered. Give me
the courage to be a loving and supportive wife
to my soul mate, even when he stumbles and
falls. May we be brought closer together as we
accept your perfect will for our lives.*

Amen.

72

The Perfect Job

By Vicki L. Julian

Pride goes before destruction, a haughty spirit before a fall.
~Proverbs 16:18

I was less than a year into my dream job of being a preschool director, but the dream was rapidly becoming a nightmare. My world was crashing, and I was the only one who knew why. It wasn't the job. It was my unrealistic expectation of what I could accomplish, and it was taking a toll on my family—especially the relationship with my husband.

Whenever a staff member did something wrong or a parent disenrolled a child, I blamed myself and took it personally. With a fifty- to sixty-hour workweek, there was little time for family. I felt like a failure at work as well as at home.

I had believed I could do it all. The words "I can't" weren't part of my vocabulary. Besides, how could I confess feeling inadequate to my wonderful husband, who had supported me at every turn? He was so proud of the awards and bonuses I earned, even though I didn't feel I deserved them. I was already letting myself down, and I simply couldn't let him down, too.

With my focus on perfection at the preschool, my husband became both mother and father to our young sons. As he gradually became weary of doing it all, we began to snap at each other. We were growing apart, and I didn't know how to stop it.

As we retired to bed one night, Steve surprised me with a question that made my heart ache. He choked out the words, "Is there someone else?" How could he even think that? I loved him so much, but now I realized that my disappointment in myself had hurt him and our children. Sobbing, I buried my face in his shoulder and admitted my perceived failures. With obvious relief, he responded as I only dared to hope—with love, support, and acceptance.

With Steve's encouragement, I met with our pastor, and his counsel helped me to again put my family first. I vowed never to forget that whatever happens, Steve and I are in it together.

Once my frailties and failures were unburdened, I didn't feel a need to leave my dream job. I remained a preschool director another seven years and was later promoted to the corporate office of the company.

I learned a valuable lesson in my quest to be perfect: "Pride goes before destruction, a haughty spirit before a fall" (Proverbs 16:18). I was blessed that my husband and my faith were both there to catch me.

My Prayer

Father in heaven, please keep me ever mindful that striving for perfection is not the same as expecting to be perfect. Help me to never let pride interfere with the focus on my family.

Amen.

Chapter 8

Devotional Stories for Wives

Second Chances

*But if you will seek God earnestly and plead with the Almighty,
if you are pure and upright, even now he will rouse himself
on your behalf and restore you to your prosperous state.*

~Job 8:5-6

Our Personal SOS

By Jeanette Levellie

Many waters cannot quench love; rivers cannot sweep it away.
~Song of Songs 8:7a

I answered the phone at work to my husband Kevin's voice, quivering and raspy. "I flipped the car over the bridge into Sugar Creek."

My knees turned to sand. "Are you okay, honey?"

"Yes. I managed to crawl out the window, up the creek bank, and walk to a neighbor's house. But the car is a mess. The police and tow truck are on their way. Can you meet me on the bridge?"

I fought to keep my voice calm in spite of my racing heart. "I'll be there as soon as I can."

After a few deep breaths to clear my muddied thoughts, I called my boss to tell him I needed to leave. On the seven-mile drive to the bridge, I searched my soul and prayed. Since moving from Los Angeles to rural Illinois a few months earlier, our lives had drifted apart. We weren't in danger of sinking. Yet.

Could this accident be an SOS for our marriage?

Half an hour later, we stood on the bridge over Sugar Creek, our arms tight around each other. We watched in silent shock as the towing crew dragged our car up the bank.

Through chattering teeth, Kevin explained what had happened.

"Just as I reached the bridge, I felt like I was driving on ice. I wrestled with the steering wheel to get control of the car." He paused, his shoulders heaving with silent sobs. "The next thing I knew, I was covered in water from my head to my waist, hanging upside down by my seatbelt. The water had come in through the open window."

My husband does not swim. If the crash had knocked him out, he'd have drowned. And because the car settled under the bridge, no one driving along would have seen him. He might have been there for days before anyone discovered him.

I shivered at the thought and looked into his eyes, clear brown and alive.

My own dripped tears into the murky water.

Not until later that night did I let myself cry freely. I sobbed my remorse to the Lord for the many times I'd been impatient with Kevin when he annoyed me or didn't live up to my expectations. I admitted how I'd taken for granted the many sweet things he did for me, like having dinner ready when I got home, grocery shopping, and pretending to like my cats. I realized how in the flash of sunlight on a bridge railing and the twist of a tire, a loved one could leave forever. I recommitted my heart to stay on board with Kevin.

They've repaired the bridge at Sugar Creek, widening it to make it safer. And every time we drive over, I breathe a thankful prayer that God gave our marriage an SOS.

My Prayer

Dear Father, you are the rescuer of sinking
lives and drowning marriages. Keep us
focused on you, so we can rise above the
waters of misunderstanding and the winds of
change. Renew our commitment to each other.

Amen.

Our Communion Table

By Cathi LaMarche

They devoted themselves to the apostles' teaching and to fellowship, to the breaking of bread and to prayer.
~Acts 2:42

The weathered table in the middle of our kitchen has been at the center of our lives over the past ten years: dinners, when our family shares successes and failures, tells jokes, and offers differing viewpoints; weekend talks with girlfriends, when we clutch our coffee cups as well as our sides while laughing and divulging secrets and crazy antics; middle-of-the-night chats with teenaged children, when their worries or algebra problems overpower sleep. Scratched and faded, yet welcoming and comfortable, the table calls our family and friends into communion, time and again.

This wasn't always the case. During my first marriage, the kitchen table was the keeper of magazines, pens, spare change, and junk mail. Frequently, I cleared a space with the swipe of my forearm to jot a note, address a letter, or balance my checkbook. The table served as a station for immediate business transactions rather than a place to share meals, tell stories, or elicit laughter. Eating our meals tucked away in the corners of separate rooms, my husband and I drifted farther and farther apart. Throughout those thirteen years, the kitchen table remained smooth and unscathed, but our marriage became bumpy and tattered. The divorce left me with feelings of failure as a wife, so I embraced the kitchen table as a single mother and shared nightly meals with my children so as not to fail at motherhood, too.

Eventually, I was offered another chance. My second husband, Michael, failed to see the value of our kitchen table since, during his previous marriage, he had dined on cold sandwiches, accompanied only by the newspaper sprawled before him. The kitchen table served as a constant reminder of his previous loneliness and floundering marriage. Meals provided sustenance with little pleasure.

Soon, our family's hot meals replaced his cold ones, and a growing stock of cookbooks lined the kitchen countertop. The evening meal became a communal event, and chatter and laughter filled the kitchen along with the scents of garlic, oregano, and thyme. Not wanting to make the same mistake the second time around, I instituted the family dinner rule despite our hectic schedule. Every night. All members. No excuses.

As a wife and mother, I now delight in listening to my husband debate politics or social issues with our son and daughter. Mealtime is a chance to discover interesting facts about ourselves and each other. As we gather around the kitchen table to break bread, we pray:

"In the name of the Father, and of the Son, and of the Holy Spirit. Amen. Bless us, oh Lord, and these thy gifts, which we are about to receive, from thy bounty, through Christ, our Lord. Amen. In the name of the Father, and of the Son, and of the Holy Ghost. The one who grabs the fastest gets the most."

And we smile.

My Prayer

*Heavenly Father, thank you for the bounty
that you so lovingly provide each night
around the dinner table. Continue to bless my
family and keep us tied together in heartfelt
fellowship with each other.*

Amen.

A Fresh Start

By Tracey L. Simpson

...stand firm in the one Spirit, striving together as one for the faith of the gospel...
~Philippians 1:27

y life reminded me of overflowing dirty laundry. Divorce, single parenting, losing our family home, and moving with my preteen son and teen daughter into cramped living quarters made me feel like a loser. The kids and I attended family counseling, but still my emotions ran high, my faith faltered, and I was full of self-doubt. When I looked at my problems, I felt like nobody would want me: not my kids, certainly not another man, and at my lowest point, not even the good Lord Himself. I felt like a castoff tossed in the corner—worn, outgrown and no longer useful.

My kids were going through typical teen angst on top of dealing with our family issues, but they had school and extracurricular activities as an outlet. When I received an invitation to my class reunion, I immediately rejected the idea. I imagined my former classmates bragging about their wonderful lives and successes, but for some reason I finally decided to attend. I was nervous when I walked in alone. I met a girlfriend, and we sat down at a table. I couldn't believe the nice guy seated next to me was David, the quiet little nerd in sixth grade who got picked on.

David and I discovered that we had a lot in common, and he asked me out. Most people have dates at a restaurant or go to a movie. We did that occasionally, but every Thursday for six months, David and I had a standing date. He'd walk up and down the grocery aisles with me as I did my weekly shopping at Walmart. We'd talk and laugh, and then he'd help me load my groceries into my car. He'd head back home twenty miles, and I would return home to my children.

On Sundays, David and I attended church. I witnessed his passion for the Word and his kindness. The patience he showed toward youngsters when we worked in the children's ministry confirmed he'd be a good father figure. As I listened to him teach the gospel messages to those little children, the words also touched my heart. I joined the church and was baptized. David and I connected on a spiritual level as well as an emotional one. We grew in the Spirit.

When we married a year later, on 10-10-10, I was a "new and improved" wife. I brought to our marriage a renewed faith in myself, my husband and, most of all, God. I felt cleansed. When I said "I do," I felt God's presence and approval. David and I were connected as one in faith, just as the Lord intends for a godly husband and wife to be.

My Prayer

*Thank you, Lord, for second chances in love.
I know your everlasting love will see me
through the dark days until I am made clean
in the image you always imagined. I am so
blessed to be a godly wife to my dear husband.*

Amen.

76

A God Thing

By Michelle Close Mills

"...For I know the plans I have for you," declares the LORD, "plans to prosper you and not to harm you, plans to give you hope and a future..."
~Jeremiah 29:11

From the moment I met Ralph, it seemed we'd always been two halves of a whole. We made it official at the wedding of our dreams, and planned for a bright and happy future. However, shortly after the honeymoon, we learned that marriage wasn't the idyllic stuff of fairy tales. Years of money troubles, job worries and raising a physically challenged child wore us out. Romance was a lovely thought, but difficult to kindle while circling the drain.

My temporary solution was to run away from home.

As often as possible.

We lived in Florida, and my folks lived in Indiana. I tried to visit them every three months or so. It was a means of escape: 1,100 miles separating me from real life.

Then, in November 1999, I received a wake-up call—an event that our pastor labeled "a God thing."

As I was boarding a flight to Indiana, I missed the last step leading toward the door of the plane, fell and twisted my ankle.

Hard.

A flight attendant helped me to my feet and offered to call for a wheelchair to take me back to the gate. I stubbornly insisted that I was fine and limped through the cabin, ignoring an inner voice that told me to get off the plane and call Ralph.

An hour after takeoff, I couldn't walk. A trip to the restroom required holding onto seat backs and hopping.

When the plane landed, Dad took me to the hospital. I had broken three bones in my foot.

Sleep that night was nearly impossible. In spite of medication, the pain was terrible. Worse yet was how foolish I felt for having made the trip.

And though I was with my loving parents, I wanted to go home. I needed my husband. In spite of our problems, Ralph was still my other half.

I returned home the following evening. When I saw Ralph's smiling face, my eyes filled with tears of relief. As he kissed me, one journey ended and another began.

The accident reminded me that home is where the heart is, and worth fighting for. I'd been so distracted by our circumstances that I could have lost the love of my life. It was time to stop running and work harder to become the partner that God intended for me to be.

I never would have imagined that a broken foot would have a hand in restoring our marriage. It truly was "a God thing."

My Prayer

Father God, when tough times arise, our first
instinct is often to run from our problems.
Please remind us to follow our hearts home
and to work harder to become the partner
you want us to be.

Amen.

77

Second Best

By Marilyn Turk

There is no fear in love. But perfect love drives out fear...
~1 John 4:18

The cheerful new mug welcomed me as I poured my morning coffee. I hoped that my "happy mug," with its hand-painted red, blue and yellow flowers and red handle, would lift me from my depression.

My husband Chuck walked into the kitchen, noticed the mug and frowned. I thought his reaction was to the smell of coffee, which he doesn't like, until he asked about the mug.

"Is that new?"

"Yes! It's my happy mug!" I held it up for him to view.

"Why did you buy another cup when we have so many dishes already?"

My mood crashed as I replied, "Because it's mine."

I fought back tears as he looked at me, bewildered. He shook his head, and then abandoned the subject as he poured his cereal. I knew his thrifty personality didn't comprehend the purchase. He didn't understand my motivation, and I couldn't explain it to him.

True, we had plenty of dishes. When we decided to get married a few months before, we had chosen which possessions we would keep from our previous marriages. We kept his blue-flowered white china, and we'd given away my dishes. It wasn't that I disliked his dishes. It was just that they were a reminder to me of his first marriage that ended when his first wife died, unlike my marriage that had ended by divorce.

We also kept his dining room and living room furniture. Although it was a mutual, rational decision, I began to feel overwhelmed by the reminders that I wasn't Chuck's first choice, despite the fact that we had bought a new home together. I loved our home—exactly what we both wanted in the neighborhood we desired. But a nagging feeling kept reminding me I wasn't his first choice, and that I'd never measure up to his first wife.

I knew I shouldn't feel that way, but I was afraid to tell Chuck what was bothering me. So I bought a new mug just to have something that was mine, not "theirs."

Yet it hadn't worked. I was running away from the problem, avoiding even the mention of her name, afraid it would make both of us uncomfortable. Finally, I decided to face my fear.

That evening, I surprised Chuck by asking him to tell me about his first wife and how they met. As I asked more questions and listened, a mental picture of the young couple formed in my mind.

He stopped, watching my response. "What else do you want to know?"

"Tell me about her illness."

With tears in his eyes, he told about the four-year battle with cancer. His pain became my pain as I listened. The barrier was down. The fear was gone. We both breathed a sigh of relief and embraced.

The next morning as I entered the kitchen, I smiled at the sunshine-yellow walls Chuck had painted for me with the white beadboard he had installed below. Looking up, I saw the painting we'd bought on our honeymoon. All around me was evidence of Chuck's love for me and our life together.

Chuck entered the room, and I said, "I need to tell you something."

"Okay." He looked worried.

With a smile, I said, "I wish I could thank Joan, because she helped you to be the man you are now."

He nodded. "You're right. She did." He leaned over and kissed me. "I love you."

"I know," I replied.

My Prayer

*Dear Father, you truly know all the healing
that we need in our lives. Thank you, God,
for staying by our sides whenever tensions
arise in our marriages. How blessed we are in
knowing that your presence always surrounds
us.*

Amen.

78

Growing in Love

By Linda C. Defew

[Love] always protects, always trusts, always hopes, always perseveres.
~1 Corinthians 13:7

M y husband and I never fell in love. There weren't any bells or whistles, no heart flutters or butter-flies in our stomachs. Still, we have a marriage many couples envy.

We knew the odds were against us. According to the statistics, sixty-seven percent of second marriages end in divorce. That's why Eddie and I knew we had to have something stronger than the unpredictable feelings of a teenager.

After a thirteen-year marriage and another thirteen years alone, my future looked bleak. I had been diagnosed with rheumatoid arthritis, a crippling disease with no cure. Within five years, my hands showed major signs of deformity. My knees swelled so badly I could hardly walk. Finally, I had to quit a job I loved. I prayed to God for a good man to come my way.

Eddie was married twenty-three years and single for eight. Despite his misery, he had stayed with his first wife until his son was eighteen. "I couldn't bear to see another man raise my child," he said. Then, just as he was getting on with his life, a gunshot wound to his left shoulder brought a disappointment maybe more devastating than the divorce. His years as a police chief were over.

A few years later, my prayers were answered. I got a phone call from Eddie asking about a tractor for sale. He explained that he was trying to call my ex-husband (whose number was listed in the phone book right under mine). When he realized his mistake, we had a good laugh, and the conversation got off on a friendlier note. Our paths had never crossed, so we had a lot to talk about. His years as Chief of Police in our small town left him with a million stories to tell.

His enthusiastic, optimistic voice lifted my spirits. I was drawn to his positive attitude and love for life. One night, he told me the details of how he nearly lost his arm and how he was still dealing with the repercussions. His honesty lifted a burden from my shoulders and made it easier for me to open up to him.

I told him all about my life, my painful divorce and the dreadful disease that followed on its heels. I explained how I was the only family member in my generation to inherit RA. My uncle and grandfather had suffered with it for years before their deaths. He listened with great interest and compassion, asking a lot of questions, but he didn't seem bothered by the prognosis.

"But I may end up in a wheelchair," I said.

He responded in his typical positive way. "So? I'll push you."

Within a few months, we were inseparable. In two years, we were husband and wife. Now, it's been sixteen years and, still, we have never fallen in love. The love we have grew day by day through deep commitment and mutually caring for one another. To me, that is the kind of love that lasts.

My Prayer

*Dear Lord, I am forever grateful for my
loving husband. You knew I needed someone
I could trust to help me through the hills and
valleys of life. Please help me to be a good
wife even on my bad days and to nurture our
commitment to love each other always.*

Amen.

79

Sticking Power

By Deanna Baird

Trust in the LORD with all your heart and lean not on your own understanding; in all your ways submit to him, and he will make your paths straight.
~Proverbs 3:5-6

From experience, I knew you could love someone and still leave. I left my husband on his birthday right after he had left for work. For months, I had been struggling with marriage, loneliness and a new baby. I wanted to bail.

My dad answered the phone that morning and told me to come home. Dad was a recovering alcoholic, and one thing I learned early and often was that when things got tough, Dad would leave. It could be for days or weeks. Sometimes we knew where he was; other times we didn't. There were job changes and moves throughout my childhood. "Sticking with it" was not something I learned a whole lot about.

Even so, that fall I searched for a way to cope. For the first time in my life, I began going to church. I struggled with the concept of the "Heavenly Father." When I heard talk about God always being with us, I thought sarcastically, "Yeah, sure He is." In my mind, it was simple. If I couldn't count on my father, how could I count on a Heavenly Father? Trusting anyone, including my husband, was difficult. With that mindset, it was no wonder my marriage proved to be a challenge. When things got tough, I left, because that's what you do.

The week at my parents' house gave me a chance to breathe. I realized I wasn't looking to end my marriage; I was looking for a way to "do" marriage. I was packing to return to my husband on January twenty-eighth, the morning the Challenger exploded. In an instant, the lives of those on the flight, their families and colleagues, changed forever. There were no more chances to change, no time to make things right. The truth of it shook me to the core. With a renewed sense of purpose, I returned to my husband and my life.

Wasting no time, I reached out in faith. And when I did, God showed me through His Word how to trust Him. His love was like nothing I had ever experienced before. That is when I learned that no one, not even my husband, could fill my deepest need. Only God could do that, and He did.

It has been thirty years, and God has shown me that it is in "staying" that life is learned. Sticking power is something God knows a great deal about.

My Prayer

Dear Lord, thank you for being the only Father I need and for sticking with me. I know that I can always count on your guidance in my life.

Amen.

With God's Help

By Wendy Hobday Haugh

May God be gracious to us and bless us and make his face shine on us—so that your ways may be known on earth, your salvation among all nations.
~Psalm 67:1-2

I was devastated when my first husband left me for someone else. But from the very start, my turbulent emotions—anger, fear, sadness and humiliation—were tempered by an unmistakable sense of relief. Suddenly, unexpectedly, I felt free to overhaul my life and become a better version of myself, more courageous and self-assured—the kind of woman and wife I'd always dreamed of being. Praying for God's guidance, I felt a flicker of hope. Somehow, I trusted I'd be okay.

With a two-year-old son and another baby on the way, I focused on motherhood, my musician's job, and making ends meet. I struggled daily with the challenges of joint custody, civility in particular, but I kept moving forward, spurred on by the unwavering belief that a better life for my growing family and me was out there somewhere.

One day, while shopping, I bumped into Chuck—an acquaintance who, like me, had recently been dumped by a loved one. Having walked down the aisle arm-in-arm with Chuck ten years earlier when my brother married his sister, we found ourselves talking easily. Chuck invited me to a beach party at his camp the following weekend. Our siblings and twin nieces would be there, he assured me. It would be fun!

On a beautiful summer day, I headed to the lake with my son. I had no intention of monopolizing Chuck's time that day, but it soon became apparent that he had every intention of monopolizing mine. He took my son exploring. He took me sailing. He played with our nieces, smiling nonstop. Later, as Chuck's soft brown eyes held mine, I was startled and awed by the thought that maybe, just maybe, this was the man God intended me to find.

"We hardly know each other!" I cried two weeks later when Chuck popped the question. "I'm not even divorced yet!" But nothing deterred him.

To my surprise, my mother was delighted to hear of Chuck's proposal, and my dad calmly remarked: "I always thought you and Chuck would make a good pair."

Although friends cautioned me against being hasty, I felt God increasingly guiding Chuck and me, encouraging us to trust in the possibility of a life together. In some ways, I barely knew him. But, inexplicably, I felt like I'd known him forever. And we shared so many common interests, family first and foremost, I could easily imagine us growing old together—something I'd never been able to envision with my ex-husband.

Without question, it was God, not chance, that brought Chuck into my life and me into his, blessing us both with the strength and conviction needed to embark on a new path. Throughout our thirty-year marriage, I've thanked the Lord daily for my gentle, loving husband, for the happier woman and wife I've become, and for the vibrant life Chuck and I have created together... with God's help.

My Prayer

Lord, bless me with your steadfast wisdom.
Help me to listen for your voice. Through
your guidance, I know that I will always try
to choose the right path for my life.

Amen.

81

Actions Speak Louder than Words

By Sara L. Schafer

*Dear children, let us not love with words or speech
but with actions and in truth.*
~1 John 3:18

I met my husband, Rick, in 1983. We were together two years before marrying. Rick and I both believe God guided us to each other. We believe it will be a marriage for a lifetime. It was fairly easy becoming a couple and a family with his two young children. There was, however, one difference that took an emotional toll on me.

I was raised in a family where we always said "I love you" before parting ways or hanging up the telephone. Rick wasn't raised that way. Each time I said "I love you" and he couldn't say it to me, it hurt. Sometimes it made me cry, and sometimes it made me angry. At times, I wondered if his inability to say three simple words would be the destruction of a marriage sanctioned by God. I thought I needed these words to be happy.

It took a couple of years of me growing spiritually and emotionally to realize the flaw was not in Rick. The flaw was in the way I was reacting to our difference. It helped to remember that from age twenty to twenty-two, I was married to another man. He said "I love you" on a daily basis, but I wasn't happy. His negative, degrading attitude toward me and our marriage was not love. His actions made his words worthless.

Rick, on the other hand, couldn't say the words, but his actions speak volumes. Through the years, he has loved me more than I ever imagined possible. He has stood by my side in triumphs and failures. He has held me as I grieved over the death of loved ones. He has laughed with me and cried with me. He was a gallant, exceptional and loving caregiver during my fight against cancer. He has been a constant source of encouragement.

After twenty-nine years, we seldom say the words "I love you," but it doesn't matter to me nor does it hurt me anymore. We show our love for each other on a daily basis through our actions and attitude toward each other. As Rick and I walk hand-in-hand, I know with this simple touch that he is saying, "I love you." I cherish each passing day with him as a gift from God.

My Prayer

Dear God, thank you for the gift of my husband. Please continue to bless us and all husbands and wives with acceptance, patience and devotion. In your Holy name, I pray.

Amen.

Chapter
9

*Devotional
Stories for
Wives*

A Change in Perspective

*"Forget the former things; do not dwell on the past. See, I am doing a
new thing! Now it springs up; do you not perceive it?"*

~Isaiah 43:18-19a

82

Driving Lesson

By Betsy Burnett

Finally, brothers and sisters, whatever is true, whatever is noble, whatever
is right, whatever is pure, whatever is lovely, whatever is admirable — if
anything is excellent or praiseworthy — think about such things.
~Philippians 4:8

While driving to worship practice one morning, I was noticing the gorgeous flowers when, oops, I drove off the road. I drove along a bit more and noticed the neighbors had added new trim to their house. Uh-oh, off the road again. "Hey, look, they changed their…" Yup, you guessed it, off the road again.

By the time I got to church, I was more than a little bewildered. I don't normally drive that poorly, so I prayed in frustration, "Lord what's going on?" That's when I heard that still, small voice in my heart say, "You'll drive toward what you focus on!"

You see, my husband had been working a lot lately. He was a truck driver who had recently switched to over-the-road driving, which meant we only saw him on weekends. When he finally did get home, all I could think about was how he hadn't been there to help with the kids or fix the washer or complete the never-ending "honey-do list." I realized I spent so much time when he was home complaining to him about not being home that I wasn't enjoying the fact he was actually there! My complaining only led to arguments, hurt feelings, and a sense of relief when he left again, only to be followed by sadness and frustration.

Right then and there, I decided to change things. Instead of driving toward the frustration of him not being home, I decided to drive toward enjoying the fact that he was home. I tried to welcome my husband home as a happy-to-see-him wife, rather than the crabby why-aren't-you-home-more version. I saved the never-ending to-do lists until I could approach him kindly, asking for help rather than telling him what I needed done. As I changed my focus, I enjoyed our time together more, and our home became a much happier place.

As time has passed, the lesson I learned that day has become invaluable. I have found that the more I focus on the positive about my husband and our marriage, the more happy I am with him, and the more content I am with our marriage. When I drive toward negative things, soon it's all I see, and it becomes easy to get angry, frustrated and bitter. This doesn't mean that I just ignore the negative, but when I focus on all that is good and kind and wonderful about my husband, it puts the negative in proper perspective, and helps me to lovingly encourage a change for the better.

My Prayer

*Dear Lord, I know I will drive toward what
I focus on. Help me to focus on the good and
admirable things that are in my husband.*

Amen.

The Comparison Trap

By Kelly Combs

We do not dare to classify or compare ourselves...
~2 Corinthians 10:12

"**W**hy can't my husband be more like her husband?" I silently wondered about a woman I knew at church. My spiritual life seemed to be growing in leaps and bounds, and yet I couldn't get my husband to do more than attend church on Sunday.

I longed to attend a Sunday school class together, but instead I attended a daytime Bible study alone, along with Mothers of Preschoolers (MOPS) and Wednesday night church dinners.

In comparison, that woman's husband seemed to be everywhere. He attended Sunday school and Wednesday night dinners with her, and sang on the praise team. He was with her and their kids at every family activity our church sponsored.

But an interesting thing happened. As I attended more events and got to be friends with her, she asked if she could share a concern with me. "My husband has anger issues, and we really need prayer," she said. I agreed to pray for her, but I was stunned. Her husband had anger issues? And I had wished my husband could be more like him...

Suddenly, I noticed all the positive things about my husband.

Yes, he "only" attended church with me, but he attended every Sunday, faithfully and without complaint. He was a kind and loving husband and father, and an excellent provider for our family. I still wished his spiritual growth would more closely mirror mine, but I no longer played the comparison game with other husbands. Instead, I focused on my husband's positive attributes and prayed for his spiritual growth.

Years passed, and eventually we changed churches. The second Sunday we attended our new church, my husband said, "I guess we should find a Sunday school class." Shocked, I just nodded and followed him down the hall. Soon, he was attending Wednesday night suppers and family events with me. I was thrilled.

This experience has taught me several lessons. First, the comparison trap is a dangerous one. Because we only see the outward appearance, we don't know what happens behind closed doors in others' homes. Not only that, but comparisons lead to bitterness and envy. In choosing to look at my husband's positive attributes, I was no longer bitter, but content.

Second, prayer works! I prayed for my husband's spiritual growth, instead of just wishing for it. But don't think it happened overnight. It was literally years before I began to see small changes, and it's been nearly ten years since we first attended our old church. But, make no mistake, God did answer my prayers on His own timetable.

I am so thankful to God for not only growing my husband, but continuing to grow me as well. Currently, my husband is working toward his master's degree in theology. I am so proud of him. When I look at my husband now, compared to the man he used to be, there is no comparison. We have both been made new by God.

My Prayer

Lord, show me what is good in my husband
and let me dwell on that. Use me to
encourage him to be the man of God that
you created him to be. Continue to bind us
together in your Holy Spirit.

Amen.

Chocolate Cake and Marriage

By Eleanor Cowles

...as far as the east is from the west, so far has he removed our transgressions from us.
~Psalm 103:12

It was to be a special Valentine's dinner. Friends were invited to bring wedding albums and special memories of their years together. I planned a salmon feast, to be crowned with a three-layer chocolate cake for dessert. I had baked this cake several times with good results. However, I was not destined for success this time.

My first problem was lack of a third cooling rack. I tried balancing the delicate cake layer on the edges of two pans, causing it to crack. Then came the cooked frosting. I misread the recipe and had only half the chocolate required. Extended cooking and the addition of powdered sugar did not thicken it.

Unwilling to give up, I placed the first layer on my pedestal cake plate. Frosting ran over the cake edge, but I added the second, and then the third layer. I tried securing the layers with metal skewers and kept pouring frosting. Finally, as it broke apart more and more,

I knew it was a losing proposition. The frosting was oozing over the cake plate onto the kitchen counter.

I cast an eye at the garbage can and was tempted. Instead, I enlisted my husband's help, and we were able to dump the entire mess into a bowl. I added the remaining frosting, stirred it a bit, and put the whole thing into the refrigerator.

I served the cake that evening with ice cream, and everyone said it was great. I showed them the recipe picture of the cake in all its glossy perfection. I compared it to marriage. In the beginning, we have a picture of how our life together will be. We forge ahead with confidence. As time passes, a few mistakes are made, and cracks appear. Sometimes, a big disaster occurs, and the cake appears ruined. At this point, we can throw away the cake or try to reshape it. The end result will not look like our beginning picture, but it may be all right. It may be even better in its altered form, if we keep our faith in God and what we have together.

My Prayer

Lord, thank you for healing the broken parts of our marriage. Help us to learn from our mistakes and to become stronger as a result.

Amen.

"Here's to my marriage: imperfect on the outside but sweet on the inside!"

Reprinted by permission of
Stephanie Piro ©2013

85

Our Emergency Communication Plan

By Julie Hornok

A person's wisdom yields patience; it is to one's glory to overlook an offense.
~Proverbs 19:11

y husband and I were eight years into our marriage and had come upon hard times. You would think with eight years under our belt, we would have had an Emergency Communication Plan in place for when times turned tough. But we didn't. And even if we had, there was no way we could have planned for this life-changing emergency.

We had recently moved into our dream home, and we were going to live there forever! The media room was top-notch, my son's room was fire-engine perfection, and I just knew our baby girl would think she was a princess in her pretty pink room.

But none of that mattered anymore; our baby girl had just been diagnosed with autism.

Over the course of months, her mind slowly went somewhere else, and we could no longer reach her. She was in her own world, and I did everything I could to pull her out. I set up thirty hours of therapy a week during the day and researched hours every night. I changed her diet, sold our house to be near a special school, and met with every autism specialist available. We were suddenly broke, my heart was broken, and I felt so alone.

Where was my husband? While I was researching cures and new therapies, my husband seemed distant. Didn't he care? Sadness turned to anger, and thoughts of the things my husband wasn't doing made me even angrier.

I let that anger separate us, and our communication grew worse. I was too exhausted to even think straight. Why couldn't he appreciate what I was doing, and why did he question every therapy I wanted to try?

In the midst of my anger, I began to pray for all the things my husband needed to do. "God, please help him be more involved in our daughter's therapy. Help him research new therapies and realize how hard I am trying to do everything."

God didn't answer my prayers the way I thought He would. Instead, He showed me that while I was doing all the therapy, doctor visits and diet changes, my husband was working long hours to pay for them! Being the sole provider for our family was a greater burden than I could ever imagine. My husband was not the one who needed an attitude change. I was.

Humbled, I let my husband know how much I loved and appreciated him. Our Emergency Communication Plan was finally activated: We were a team, and with God's help, we would together face the long road ahead for our daughter.

My Prayer

Dear God, thank you for all that my husband does daily to show his love to me and our family. Please give me wisdom and patience, so that I can overlook any offense that comes my way. Show me how I can be a better wife to him. In your name, I pray.

Amen.

86

I Will Remember Your Name

By Janice Flood Nichols

...for the LORD will be at your side and will keep your foot from being snared.

~Proverbs 3:26

"**S**ir, are you deployed?"

"Yes," replied my husband.

Intently focused on the medical corps' caduceus prominently displayed on my husband's Army fatigue collar, signifying that he was a physician, Private Garcia responded: "Then I will remember your name. I may need you."

As I watched the enlisted soldier, twenty years old at best, salute my husband and quickly disembark the Fort Dix transport bus, my eyes filled with tears.

You see, I had never been placed in a position where I had to "share" my husband beyond the familiar territory of local emergency rooms. I was used to middle-of-the-night and weekend interruptions, but I had always known where Dave was, a few miles from home.

Having received a deferment to attend medical school during the Viet Nam era, Dave had had no contact with our military services until the spring before Iraq invaded Kuwait. Asked to join the Reserves, Dave had chosen an Army commission. Though my husband had accepted his new professional commitment without reservation, I had been on edge. I had signed on to be the wife of a guy ruled by "Mistress Medicine," but how would I ever cope if my husband was sent into harm's way?

On a chilly mid-November morning in 1990, I received the call I had long dreaded: "Major Nichols must report to Fort Dix in seventy-two hours."

Though Dave departed for New Jersey in less than three days, our son Kevin and I were given sufficient time to fly to the post for an additional round of hugs and tears. I must admit that, at the time, I felt little patriotic fervor. I was furious with my husband, the Army, Saddam Hussein, and the world! I couldn't shake my feelings until I looked into the eyes of Private Garcia. I saw someone little more than a boy, someone's son, someone's boyfriend perhaps, yet someone willing to go into battle, asking little more than a simple guarantee that if he was injured, doctors and nurses would be there to care for him.

Only then was I able to appreciate that my husband did not "belong" to me. I finally accepted that I had to let go and let God give my husband the unfettered support he deserved. I learned what military sacrifice truly meant, not only for the soldiers, but also for fearful families at home.

Thankfully, my husband returned from Saudi Arabia six months later. Soon after, the war ended. I scanned a list of soldiers who had been killed in action; fortunately, Private Garcia's name was not among the fallen.

But, Private Garcia, I will always remember your name. You expected so little, but taught me so much about being a wife, a partner.

My Prayer

*Dear God, please give me the grace and
courage to not hold tight to those I love, but
to give them the freedom to fly unimpeded
toward their dreams and destinies.*

Amen.

87

Falling in Like

By Jeni Bullis

A wife of noble character who can find? She is worth far more than rubies.
Her husband has full confidence in her and lacks nothing of value. She brings
him good, not harm, all the days of her life.
~Proverbs 31:10-12

y husband and I attended a marriage conference after we had been married for a couple of years. It was a great weekend of intense conversations and the chance to focus on each other without distractions or interruptions.

At one session, we were asked to stand and share our favorite thing about our spouse. Each person described some trait or characteristic about their beloved that they liked the most. I stood and gushed about my admirable and amazing husband. Then it was his turn. He said, "What I like best about my wife is that... she really likes me."

Silence. I smiled, but my face turned red with anger and embarrassment.

Later, I tore into him.

"Seriously? What you like best about me is that I like you? How could you take a moment meant to be about me and make it about you?"

Of course, he was crushed. He apologized for hurting me. I forgave him, and we moved on with the weekend.

But I revisited that incident in my mind over and over for years. How could he say that? Is it that hard to come up with something that he likes about me? He is such a loving and giving husband, so where did that self-centered comment come from?

Slowly, I began to understand what was in the heart of my husband. And what my reaction did to him.

Before marrying me, my husband had gone through the worst kind of rejection. He was betrayed by a wife who chose to walk away from their marriage. And while they were married, she was disrespectful and did not make him a priority.

I also began to notice other marriages and how wives would berate and mistreat their husbands, rolling their eyes at their husbands' comments or correcting them as though they were children in front of friends and family. Some wives would call them names and make fun of them. They would complain about their sex lives and behave as though making love to their husband was a chore that they might choose to endure if he behaved just right.

As I grew in understanding of how men think, and how they process life, I recalled something about that incident at the marriage conference. When my husband had said what he did, I remember noticing every man in that room smiling as if to say, "Man, you're lucky."

Now I count it a great compliment that he is blessed by how much I like him. And I understand that it isn't selfishness that prompts him to enjoy that part of me. It's his way of acknowledging the "good thing" that comes with a loving wife.

My Prayer

Lord, help me to be a wife who is a blessing to her husband each day. Help me to love him as you would, and live in such a way that others see your work and glorify you.

Amen.

Uniquely Perfect

By Brittany Valentine

Every good and perfect gift is from above, coming down from the Father of
the heavenly lights, who does not change like shifting shadows.
~James 1:17

I can remember the sound of the door shutting as my husband's father left. The noise pierced the silence in our tiny apartment. Having just driven halfway across the country to move us to seminary, he was anxious to get back home. As the last sliver of hallway light faded and our door was locked, my heart sank. We had absolutely nothing but each other, and shortly a new baby. Overwhelmed and lonely, I fought back tears, trying to support my husband in this new adventure.

Days of unemployment grew into weeks, and weeks into months. Various stresses seemed to overcome the once peaceful trust we felt, and our marriage became a crazy cycle of arguing and irritation. I wish I could say it only lasted a few weeks, but honestly this cycle went on for a few years.

Our schedules became crazy. Having left two full-time jobs, we found ourselves working four to five jobs between the two of us just to pay bills. Then, the birth of our son took us down to just one income. We tried somewhat to make our marriage more bearable—and at times things were better—but it didn't last long.

One morning nearly three years into our marriage, I sat pouring out my heart to the Lord. I could hear as He whispered into my heart, "Perhaps he isn't the only one who needs to change." Almost instantly, the Lord radically transformed my thinking about my husband. He spoke powerfully to me through James 1:17, "Every good and perfect gift is from above, coming down from the Father of the heavenly lights, who does not change like shifting shadows."

God created my husband perfectly for me, not perfect. His strengths perfectly complement my weaknesses and I am a better wife and mother because of who God created him to be. All those years I spent consumed with frustration over my marriage because of my unmet expectations could have easily been avoided had I just been willing to remove the plank from my own eye, and seek God wholeheartedly about changing my heart. The transformation within my heart was overwhelming, and the Lord's mercy in my marriage relationship was nothing short of spectacular. My husband loves Jesus, and thankfully in spite of myself, my husband loves me. As the walls of self-righteousness and frustration tumbled down, God brought restoration and healing. Perhaps God was using the years of frustration to draw me nearer to Him. He was showing me that a "perfect" marriage isn't one without arguments or occasional dissension, but rather one that reflects the love of Christ, which itself embodies forgiveness, grace and peace.

My Prayer

*Father, help me to trust in your rich mercy
and grace. The spouse you have chosen for
me may not be perfect, but is perfectly fitted
for me. Help me to love and honor you in
loving and honoring my spouse.*

Amen.

89

Don't forget to Laugh

By Janeen Lewis

She is clothed with strength and dignity; she can laugh at the days to come.
~Proverbs 31:25

The snow drifted around the tires of my mysteriously dead Honda. After it failed to start several times, I asked my husband to work on the car. Wrapped in a big coat, Jesse stamped his boots at the front door after installing a new battery. He shook his head in defeat and rubbed his chapped hands.

"I don't know what's wrong with it."

"I'll have it towed," I said. But we were both worried. We were on a tight budget, and if the car couldn't be repaired, replacing it would be costly.

The next day, after a shiny red tow truck whisked away my car, I waited impatiently for the mechanic to call. Finally, I called him.

"Did you find out what was wrong with my car?" I asked.

"Yep," he said, with a matter-of-fact confidence.

"Is it going to be expensive?" I closed my eyes and braced myself.

"It'll cost you five dollars," he answered. "That's how much gas I put in it."

The mechanic's laughter was the only thing greater than my relief. When Jesse got home from work, I couldn't wait to tell him.

"Great news, honey! The car doesn't need a major repair. It was just out of gas!"

Maybe it was my imagination, but Jesse didn't seem pleased.

"Do you mean to tell me that I put a one-hundred-dollar battery in the car, and you had it towed because it was out of gas?" he said.

"Well, if you want to be a pessimist about it," I muttered. But deep down, I was immediately sorry for my costly mistake.

For the next hour, our home was deafeningly silent. The snow fell, the wind howled, and I felt a cold draft. That is precisely the moment when God showed me that laughter is good medicine.

As I stood in the hall adjusting the thermostat, I could feel Jesse's presence next to me. He spoke with lightness in his voice.

"Do you need help, honey? A thermostat is a little more complicated than a gas gauge."

Jesse's words sliced through the tension, and I melted into his arms. We both laughed and laughed. Even though the "empty tank" episode happened years ago, we still laugh about it today.

After that incident, God blessed me with two pieces of wisdom. First, in marriage it is important to keep your laughter tank full — life gets too serious if we forget to laugh. Maybe that is why the wife of noble character in Proverbs 31 could "laugh at the days to come." Second, and just as important, I learned to always, always check the gas gauge before having the car towed!

My Prayer

Dear Lord, thank you for reminding me that laughter is good medicine. Help me to take a daily dose of it, and continue to show my husband and me the merriment in our marriage so that our bond will grow stronger.

Amen.

Reprinted by permission of
Stephanie Piro ©2013

90

Attitude Adjuster

By Beverly LaHote Schwind

"Honor your father and mother"—which is the first commandment with a promise—"so that it may go well with you and that you may enjoy long life on the earth."
~Ephesians 6:2-3 (NKJV)

"**W**ould you like to come here and live?" I asked over the phone.

"Yes," she sobbed.

I couldn't believe the words coming out of my mouth as I invited my mother-in-law to live with us. Lillian had never considered me good enough to marry her son. We were now retired and lived five hundred miles away from her home. She had visited, on occasion, with other family members. Now due to her age and ailing health, she needed help. I could not resist her pleading. My husband and I had discussed the possibility of her coming, but he had left the decision up to me.

When I was little, my mom had brought her mother-in-law to live with us. The son she lived with had gone into the Army. As a child, I enjoyed having Grandma there, but knew it was not always easy on my mother.

We moved Lillian into our home. She was pleased with her bedroom and the way I had furnished it.

"Help me keep my focus on you, Lord," I prayed, as the changes started taking place in our home. I knew this would not be easy, as Lillian had never really accepted me, but I understood her feelings for her son. It was not about me, but about her not wanting to share her only child with anyone. I learned to go into my bedroom almost every day and pray, "Lord, please change my attitude so I can be the kind of woman I should be. Help me show love."

At times, it was tense between the two of us. I wanted to honor her even though I was upset. My husband poured out his love for me as I struggled. God let me know that He had faith in me to go on this journey.

The grandchildren enjoyed having a grandma near them. She liked playing games. It was a happy time for her, and I saw the person she wanted to be through the grandchildren. I honored her as the mother of my husband.

At night, my husband and I shared the events of the day. This had become a vital part of our marriage through the fifty years. Many times we would end up laughing at situations that seemed ugly at first. I realized, as I was tested almost daily, that God had strengthened me.

As the years passed, Lillian eventually told me she loved me. I grew to be glad she had come to live with us. I learned how to share my husband with his mother and not make her feel excluded. At one time, we may have been two women competing for the love of one man, but all along there was enough love for all. God is an attitude adjuster; all we have to do is ask Him.

My Prayer

*Dear Lord, thank you for loving me so much
that you take a negative thought and turn
it into a positive word. I pray that you will
continue to nurture all the relationships in
my life. Help me each day to find humor in
situations that seem frustrating and always
remain in your loving service.*

Amen.

91

Chicken Soup for the Soul®

The Joy of Giving

By Kay Conner Pliszka

For the Word that God speaks is alive and full of power...
~Hebrews 4:12

My husband and I recently celebrated our fortieth wedding anniversary. Before our marriage, friends had jokingly said, "It's never going to last."

Mike and I are as different as night and day. He is a neat freak who throws out all but necessities. I keep everything. He is a sports fanatic. I am not. He would rather be home alone watching TV. I would rather entertain friends. Mike hates being around children. I love kids. But the biggest challenge comes because I am a Christian and he is not.

When Mike was young, he was an altar boy with dreams of becoming a priest. Unfortunately, now he is bitter about religion. This breaks my heart because I am deeply invested in my faith.

When, in the past, he questioned my beliefs, even if sarcastically, I did my best to explain. And I rejoiced that he was at least being inquisitive. For years, I have suggested he direct his questions to one of the ministers of my church. But he won't do that. His questions are difficult. Why do bad things happen to good people? Why do some folks who call themselves Christians act improperly? How can I believe in a God who is invisible? How does one explain blind faith?

It seems, though, that most of our quibbles center on my time or money spent on others. Mike doesn't care if I spend money on myself or on family or if I spend time on something I enjoy. He just doesn't get that giving my time and money for others in need is what Christians do.

A few months ago, Mike came to church because I was singing a solo. The minister talked about tithing. He quoted the Bible, saying: "What good will it be for someone to gain the whole world, yet forfeit their soul?" (Matthew 16:26).

Since then, when Mike gets upset because he feels I'm giving too much of my time or money to a church or community project, I no longer even try to explain. I just quietly repeat, "What good will it be for someone to gain the whole world, yet forfeit their soul?"

After forty years, I have finally found the one way to stop Mike's angry questions on this subject—no explanations, no frustrating replies, no arguments, just powerful words from the Bible. And then there is silence.

I think in his heart Mike wants to have faith, to believe in a God of love and to understand my joy. I pray for him every day. But I know that the most important thing I can do is to show my husband patience and kindness and my great love for God.

Perhaps, through my words and actions, one day Mike, too, will come to know my Jesus and the joy of giving.

My Prayer

Dear Lord, please help me to be more Christ-like. When I am confronted with anger, help me to remain calm. Let me counter intolerance with patience and return arrogance with humility.

Amen.

92

My Happiness, His Gravy

By Holli Pearson

Truly my soul finds rest in God; my salvation comes from him. Truly he is my
rock and my salvation; he is my fortress, I will never be shaken.
~Psalm 62:1-2

s a new wife, thirty-two years ago, I was startled and very upset with my brand-new husband when he said, "Holli, I am not in charge of your happiness. You are!" That statement almost ended our marriage until it was explained.

Steve said, "You have to be able to make your own happiness. Don't lay that responsibility on me."

You see, as a newlywed, I thought he would want to spend every waking moment with me. I discovered that not only did my husband love to hunt and fish, but he would also be traveling because of his business. I was in a new city with a new job, and had no friends or family around. I wanted my husband to help me. I wanted him to make it all better and make me happy. The problem with that was he was busy making a living and pursuing the interests that had always been a part of his life.

I guess I could have tried to develop a love for hunting and fishing, but they didn't really interest me. The problem with our marriage was that we needed to learn to be responsible for own happiness while growing together as a couple. We needed to pursue new interests together, but also independently. This was new territory for me, but I realized it was necessary for our marriage to work.

So I developed a love of reading that has enabled me to go fishing and hunting with Steve when he asks. This hobby kept my mind occupied and my brain working throughout the years of raising children. My love of reading led to becoming a Bible Study leader, which helped me acquire a deeper faith and a firm foundation for our marriage and family.

Now when I tell my classes this story, I repeat Steve's "down home" compliment to me when he says, "You are the gravy on my mashed potatoes." That's a great analogy when describing the way our marriage works. We are each in charge of our own happiness, while finding mutual happiness in completing each other.

My Prayer

Dear Lord, you are my joy and my strength.
Help me to find my happiness in you and not
lay that burden on my husband. May we find
the perfect balance between our own interests
and those we share together.

Amen.

Chapter

10

Devotional

Stories for

Wives

Together in Strength

I can do all this through him who gives me strength.

~Philippians 4:13

93

The Tie That Binds

By Alice King Greenwood

...A cord of three strands is not quickly broken.
~Ecclesiastes 4:12

I woke up on a crisp December day in 1944 as excited as any girl could be. This was my wedding day! The preparations were complete. Mother had finished my wedding gown a week earlier. My brother picked up the flowers at the florist. The cake, silverware, and punch set looked lovely on the table of our dining room, ready for the reception following the ceremony.

Walking down the aisle, I kept my eyes on the groom. Morris looked so handsome in his black suit. My bridesmaids wore pastel-colored dresses and carried bouquets of matching flowers. The groomsmen lent a wartime aura to the occasion as they stood clad in uniforms that represented almost every branch of military service. Everything was perfect.

After the wedding and reception, I donned my special "going-away suit," and we left for our honeymoon. Our plan was to spend the first night in a town two hours away before continuing to our final destination. Out on the road, Morris heeded his father's last words: "Remember to keep both hands on the steering wheel!"

All went well for a while, but suddenly we realized one of the tires was going flat. Oh, those old retread tires! They were all we could get during the war, and they were not dependable. With a groan of disgust, we got out of the car into the cold night air. Morris opened the trunk, pulled out the jack and spare (another retread), and began, with difficulty, to try to change the tire. I said a silent prayer for success.

Soon, a car full of laughing, noisy teenagers on their way home from a party came down the highway. To our amazement, they stopped and asked if we needed help. In no time at all, the strong young men had our car jacked up, the flat tire off, and the spare mounted. What a Godsend!

Arriving at the hotel much later than planned, we checked into our room, both exhausted from the events of the day. It was then that my new husband gave me the most valuable gift a bride could receive. It was not a tangible thing wrapped with shiny paper and ribbons. Instead, it was a demonstration of the kind of person he was, his character honed by his devotion to God, and the reason, I am sure, God had brought us together.

"Let's read from my Bible," he said as he opened it to the book of Genesis, "a chapter every night." Afterwards, we knelt by the side of the bed, held hands, and prayed, asking God to guide and bless our new life together.

Thus began a practice that continued throughout our sixty-two years of marriage. At the end of each day, we confirmed our trust in God's care as we communed with Him. He was the stabilizing anchor in our lives. God was the third strand in the cord that bound us together as one.

My Prayer

*Father, I praise you for the wonderful way
you have worked everything together for the
good in my life, as you promised. Thank you
for the blessed trinity that is alive and well in
my marriage today.*

Amen.

94

Are You a Runner?

By Joanne Kraft

*"...I would flee far away and stay in the desert; I would hurry
to my place of shelter, far from the tempest and storm."*
~Psalm 55:7-8

Are you a runner? I sure am. No, I'm not talking about
the type of runner who throws her legs over the side of
the bed every morning and laces up her running shoes
to dance a while on a concrete stage. I'm talking about
the runners who flee when anything tough comes their way—escapees from their prison of pain.

My earliest memory of running is from childhood when my little
brother accidentally stepped on my toe. That was all it took. I bolted
out of our house, slamming our white aluminum screen door behind
me as I ran down the street. I couldn't bear to have my family watch
me cry from the pain.

When I was enormously pregnant with my second child, I recall
having an argument with my husband. In minutes, I was out the door
and in my car. Before long, I found myself alone in the middle of a
movie theater with tears softly plopping into my bucket of buttered
popcorn.

Over the years, I've learned to curb my running habit. No longer
do I run out the front door every time I'm hurt. But I have been

known to walk to the other side of the house or scoot to the far side of the bed. It's easy to let a five-minute argument blossom into a weekend event. Leaving the scene of the crime has never been helpful. It only prolongs the reconciliation process.

My husband and I are spiritual late-bloomers. When we became Christians, we learned for the first time that God's Word is the blueprint for a healthy and happy marriage. Marriage is God's plan. He created it. So, who better to fix it when it's broken?

I wouldn't take my car problems to my hairstylist or my computer problems to my dentist. So, why was I taking my marriage problems to my single girlfriend, my unhappily married coworker or Oprah?

I learned early on that running is unhealthy for a marriage. Throughout the years, there will be times of disagreement, and pain is sometimes inevitable. Fleeing from it isn't always the best answer. Meeting it head-on is difficult, but so worth it.

It's been a very long time since I've run. My running shoes are packed up and put away. I'm not sure I could find them if I tried. Today, I know the One who can make my marriage healthy and strong. And until He calls me home, the only place I plan on running is into the open arms of my husband.

My Prayer

Dear Lord, only you can provide shelter from the storms of life. When problems arise, may I remember not to run from them, but to turn them over to you.

Amen.

95

The Gift of Dance

By Mary C. M. Phillips

Then young women will dance and be glad, young men and old as well.
I will turn their mourning into gladness; I will give them comfort
and joy instead of sorrow.
~Jeremiah 31:13

"One, two, three. One, two, three." My husband and I are taking ballroom dancing lessons. It was his idea. No joke.

Our friends had registered a few months ago with a local dance instructor and the husband sent an e-mail to several dozen couples asking if anyone might be interested in joining them.

I remember glancing at the message and pressing "delete," knowing Mark would never consider dancing lessons—let alone ballroom dancing lessons.

But… I was wrong.

A few minutes later (as he, too, received the message), I opened an e-mail from him that read, "This looks like fun. Do you want to sign up?"

I had to check the sender's name to make sure this was, in fact, from my husband. My non-dancing husband. This could not be from the same man who sits beside me at weddings as I pout and plead, "Please dance with me," when the DJ plays a good song.

This could not be the same man who rolls his eyes when I finally, exasperated, invite another woman (who also has a non-dancing husband) to join me on the dance floor.

But it is. One and the same.

We've now learned five different moves—the last being the "big move" where I unravel out from his arms, then curl back in and raise one leg up and out, placing my entire body weight onto him.

When the instructor showed us the "big move," I refused to do it at first. Reluctantly, after some encouragement I agreed to attempt it, but was afraid to place my full weight onto my husband, fearing I'd fall. The instructor demonstrated it several times, but it made no difference to me—she's all of a size 4, if that! "Of course, he can support her," I thought. "I'm a different story."

I had to place my full trust in my husband. "I promise I won't let you fall," he said.

The other two couples gave it a shot, and it worked for them. So I took a deep breath and submitted.

My husband was like a rock, like an oak with roots. I placed every bit of my weight on him, trusting in his words, and gave it my all.

Out of the corner of my eye, I saw our reflection in the corner mirror as I raised my left leg, pointed toe and all, toward the ceiling. We looked beautiful and graceful.

We were really dancing!

I never would have suspected that ballroom dancing lessons would have such a positive effect on our marriage. But dancing with my husband gives me such joy. I love being close to him, looking into his eyes, and trusting his lead as I submit to each move.

So much of it depends on trust... and eye contact. You need to look in each other's eyes as you dance. And I can tell you, after twenty-five years of marriage, there were many days when we had stopped doing that.

Waltz Night has become our favorite night of the week, when my husband and I share the gifts of music, friends, and love.

It doesn't get any better than that.

And I hope this dance never ends.

My Prayer

Lord God, thank you for sending me a loving partner. As my husband and I learn to dance together through the trials and joys of marriage, help us to trust in each other, just as we trust in you to lead the way.

Amen.

96

Learning to Be a Helper

By Lisa Littlewood

The LORD God said, "It is not good for the man to be alone.
I will make a helper suitable for him."
~Genesis 2:18

t was an ordinary, chaotic weekday morning. A floral canvas
lunch box needed to be filled, breakfast needed to be served,
backpacks needed to be packed, hair and teeth awaited
brushing, and clothing had to be properly picked out and put
on—all in time to get our older daughter, who was in kindergarten,
to the bus, and our younger to her preschool class on time.

In other words, as usual, the needs of my children were far more
pressing than those of anyone else in the house.

"The children need to be eating in two minutes!"

"They need to be dressed in fifteen. The bus comes in twenty!"

In the midst of scrambling eggs and buttering toast for our two
girls, my husband often finds a moment to fix me a cup of coffee, cut
a grapefruit into sections, or make me an egg sandwich for the road.

"Here you go, babe," he'll say as he slides them across the counter
to his manic lunch-making wife.

I am embarrassed to confess that not only do I do no such thing in return, but I often forget to even offer a "thank you."

Then, one day, last winter, I reread a scripture in the book of Genesis that really impacted the way I started to think about things. "The LORD God said, 'It is not good for the man to be alone. I will make a helper suitable for him' (Genesis 2:18)."

A helper? Perhaps, in the early years of dating and marriage, I strived to help, but in the six years since becoming parents, "help" had become such a large part of taking care of the girls that there seemed to be little time or energy left for helping my husband in tangible ways. If anything, most days left me asking for help from him rather than offering help to him.

Several days after reading that passage, I decided to do something that would surprise him. I made him a toasted peanut butter and jelly sandwich and ran outside (in the snow!) to start his car while he was getting dressed.

As he came flying down the stairs to head out the door to his morning sales appointment and raced to find his keys, I smiled and said, "They're in your car. I started it for you."

Stopped in his tracks, he looked at me with raised eyes and a confused grin.

"Really?"

"Yes. Really. And there is some toast wrapped for you to take on the road."

"For me?" He almost laughed. "Where did you come from?"

The question was well deserved. While there are many times I have wanted to be a helper to him, I have allowed the needs of our children to take priority over the needs of my husband, leaving him to fend for himself.

I'm realizing that, even in the midst of the busyness of raising small children, I can be more deliberate about finding small ways to help him.

When I am being a "helper," even in the midst of the mayhem, I am not only serving him, but HIM—the Heavenly Father who brought us together in the first place.

My Prayer

Dear Heavenly Father, thank you for my husband. I pray that you will show me ways to be his helper today. Please forgive me for the ways that I have neglected his needs, and give me the strength and energy I need to be a good mother and wife.

Amen.

"Love is a warmed up car and breakfast on the go!"

Reprinted by permission of
Stephanie Piro ©2013

In Sickness and in Health

By Brenda Louque

Husbands, love your wives, just as Christ loved the church
and gave himself up for her...
~Ephesians 5:25

On a Saturday morning in September 2011, I woke up with a low-grade fever and a nagging ache in my lower back. My husband drove me to the emergency room because I thought I had a kidney infection, but my diagnosis would not be that simple. No antibiotic would cure my problem.

After the urinalysis came back negative, the emergency room doctor ordered a CT scan. He seemed to think I had a kidney stone. I will never forget the look on the doctor's face when he gave me the results. His face was lined with pity when he said to me, "The CT scan indicates lymphoma."

I was sent home with instructions to call my family physician on Monday. My husband held my hand all the way and kept telling me that I was going to be okay. I sat in stunned silence, not believing the diagnosis.

The diagnosis, however, was correct. After having bone marrow and lymph node biopsies, I was determined to have Type B non-

Hodgkin's lymphoma. It is a slow-growing lymphoma, but I was already in stage 4. My husband was the one to ask questions, while I sat in shocked silence. He was the one who assured me that my hair wouldn't fall out, and if it did, he would buy me "new hair."

The coming months were to be some of the hardest in our lives. My husband became my tower of strength. He drove me to all my appointments. He held my hand during my first round of chemo. He cooked meals that I "thought" I wanted, but was too nauseated to eat. He prayed with me and for me when I was too sick to pray for myself.

He became my nurse, housekeeper, and sole breadwinner. He gave up golf dates and fishing trips to stay home with me. Many times, he has told me, "I don't want to go to work and leave you because I worry about you."

He has been by my side every step of the way through my cancer journey. He has held me when I cried in frustration and encouraged me when I wanted to give up. And he was there when I got the news that my lymphoma was in remission.

When I try to tell him how much I appreciate him, he just says, "I am trying to be the man that God wants me to be."

Thank you, Lord, for this man. By your mercy and grace, and with my husband's love, I have conquered my disease.

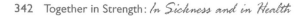

My Prayer

Almighty Father, I am so thankful for my husband, my tower of strength, here on Earth. Continue to let your light shine upon us as we move through our life together. Let us all strive to be the men and women of God you want us to be.

Amen.

98

He Must Be Greater

By Pamela Louise Walker

"…He must become greater; I must become less."
~John 3:30

I have always loved old, traditional things and I wanted my wedding to reflect that. I chose to go with the age-old "love, honor and obey" when I pledged my "troth." I didn't really know what those words meant; I just knew they felt right. It's taken almost a quarter of a century to fully understand just how "right" they are.

At first, marriage was everything I had dreamed of and more. My new husband showered me with cards, flowers and little gifts to show he was thinking of me. Over the years, the tokens of his affection gradually slowed down and eventually stopped coming altogether. A lifetime of things—stress at work, job loss, the birth and raising of special-needs children, and aging parents moving in with us—took their toll on our happily ever after.

Time didn't, however, erase my need for those things. I left hints and even came right out and asked, but my requests seemed to fall on deaf ears. I knew he loved me, but I couldn't figure out why he didn't want to give me what I desired most. I tried to do whatever he wanted and needed. I cooked his favorite meals. I washed his clothes. Shouldn't he give me what I needed to feel loved?

I began to resent him and all I felt I was expected to do. I let laundry and dishes pile up. I let housekeeping go. I went to bed before him so I didn't have to kiss him goodnight. Our house and our life began to fall apart, and neither of us seemed to be willing to do something about it. One day after an especially tearful prayer, I picked up my Bible and came across John 3:30. More of Him, less of me.

Those words spoke directly to my heart, and I was forever changed. I was not looking at marriage the right way. Marriage is not just about us; it's about God, too. I wasn't trying to honor God in my marriage. I wanted my actions to make my husband feel obligated to give me what I wanted. God had little to do with the equation.

I made a decision that day to make it less about me and more about God. It's not always an easy thing to do, but consciously putting God first has made all the difference in our marriage. The flowers and cards have reappeared. Our home is slowly becoming the haven it should be, and we always try to remember to kiss goodnight. We both feel loved.

Life isn't a fairy tale… it's real. It will always have its ups and downs. Don't forget you are not in this alone. Do your best to "love, honor and obey" God by making it more about Him and less about you, and He will give you strength to weather whatever life throws your way. He will always love you. That's a promise you can depend on.

My Prayer

Dear God, I really want to get this right!
Teach me today to make my marriage less
about me. Show me new and wonderful ways
to offer my husband true gifts of the heart.

Amen.

99

Two Hearts

By Debbie Acklin

Wait on the LORD; Be of good courage, and He shall strengthen your heart;
Wait, I say, on the LORD!
~Psalm 27:14 (NKJV)

It was Valentine's Day. Home from work, I headed toward the bedroom, looking for my husband. The sight of two pink chocolate-filled hearts on the bed stopped me in the doorway. My husband turned to face me with a grin. He had been a casualty of employee cutbacks at his job and out of work for a few weeks. Our cash flow had become severely restricted, so we were budgeting carefully. The two small gifts—one for me and one for our daughter—were an extravagance. I felt a wave of nausea come over me as I realized that my news would soon overshadow the sweetness of this thoughtful gesture.

With a heavy heart, I entered the room. Leaning against the dresser, I stood silently with my coat still on, my purse in hand. My eyes brimmed with tears, and my husband's smile sagged into a frown. His blue eyes clouded.

"I just lost my job," I blurted out as the tears began to flow.

"What happened?" he asked, panic in his voice.

My heart cracked. Dropping my purse, I slid slowly down the front of the dresser. Falling to my knees, I wept uncontrollably.

"Debbie, what happened?" he asked again, my silence panicking him even more.

I lifted my face and looked at him. "They didn't need me anymore. Last one in, first one out," I said through my tears. "I have a severance check in my purse, and my personal belongings are still on the back seat of the car."

Dropping to the bed, he barely missed the pink hearts he had so lovingly placed there. For the next half-hour, I relayed the events of the day. His shoulders drooped under the burden I had just placed there. In the end, I sat on the floor, a red-eyed, tear-stained mess, repeating "I'm so sorry."

My husband had soldiered through each day, searching for another job, reviewing our finances, keeping a brave face to steady the family, but I always knew he was hanging on by a thread. I knew my news would only increase the burden on his heart. Finally, he said, "Well, God has always taken care of us in the past. We just need to trust Him now." He pulled me to my feet, and we held each other. Later, we sat down together and restructured our budget, adjusting for my severance check.

A few months later, we both found jobs, and life returned to normal. I must admit, I still cannot look fondly on that Valentine's Day, but now when my life feels out of control, I remember the two pink candy hearts. They remind me of God's faithfulness to strengthen our two hearts as we supported one another and aspired to "be of good courage" while we waited upon the Lord.

My Prayer

Dear Lord, I pray for myself, and every wife, that you would always give us the strength to stand in the face of adversity, and that you would provide us with the love and courage of a godly husband to stand with us.

Amen.

I finally See Him

By MJ Wagner

"My grace is sufficient for you, for my power is made perfect in weakness."
~2 Corinthians 12:9

My perception of men had been altered because of my upbringing. I grew up with a belief that all men had a temper and were to be feared. So I built up walls. In my marriage, I had always kept my husband at a distance, never wanting him to get too close emotionally. I acted like the strong one in the household because I felt safer that way.

We had been married for ten years when a health crisis left me unable to do anything physical for the better part of three years. My husband had to take care of everything, including me. I hated myself because I couldn't be the woman I used to be. I liked feeling in control, but I could no longer control anything. I felt so useless, but my husband just kept saying, "I love you, and that's all that matters. Don't give up. I'll take care of you."

Even though he said this repeatedly, it took me a long time to believe him. I had never really trusted him until I was brought to this place of vulnerability and was forced to see him as he really is: my protector, comforter, and best friend.

Through those difficult years, God showed me that I had had a distorted view of my husband. I learned that my husband was both strong and gentle. He was wise enough to understand my deepest fears and strong enough to take care of things when my physical health became compromised.

I had closed off so much of myself that when he needed to take care of me physically, I didn't know how to accept this new role. However, I noticed something happening inside of me. My husband said, "You're nicer and kinder than you used to be."

Up until that point, I hadn't realized I had been hard on him. But my eyes were opened in a way that made me know God was working a miracle in our marriage. He knew I needed a man with a soft touch, but that I couldn't receive it until I was brought to a place where I had nowhere else to look but to my husband. And when I did, all I saw was the heart of God.

My Prayer

*Lord, thank you for your hand that is at work
in our marriage. Please allow me to always
see your loving heart beating in my husband.
Cause me to be aware and grateful that you
are with me through him and that he is my
helper as much as I am his.*

Amen.

We Always Have Spring

By Ann Elizabeth Robertson

The land produced vegetation: plants bearing seed according to their kinds and trees bearing fruit with seed in it according to their kinds. And God saw that it was good.
~Genesis 1:12

I love all the seasons, even winter. Well, at least the holiday months of winter. Anything after Christmas could easily be dropped from my calendar.

One year, spring came very late. The first Saturday morning we could finally work outside my list of chores seemed endless. Already exhausted, I whispered a simple prayer, "Lord, help me see your beauty in this day, the simple pleasures of life in you."

Thirty minutes later, my husband Bill called me outside. His clothes were covered with dirt and flecks of leaves from raking.

"Come with me, Ann. I have to show you something."

We edged down the slope behind our house to the stand of bird feeders.

"Look," Bill said, pointing to the ground. Covering the hill were tender green lines of leaves, gently caressing tiny wild strawberries. They were a painting of life, lovely and delicate.

"Now come see this," Bill said, catching my hand to guide me around the shrubs behind our patio. There before us was a thick row of irises—curling pink velvet petals with stems long and leaning, most regally posed. We stood quietly at first. For the thirteen years we'd lived here, this was the first spring those irises had ever bloomed.

"I'm guessing the bulbs were rearranged last summer when the irrigation system was placed," Bill reasoned.

"All this time," I said, "this area possessed immense beauty. And it was lying dormant, simply needing to be positioned for such a time as this."

Bill and I stood arm in arm, receiving the sweet gift of God now revealed.

Remember what has been planted within you and your husband, both individually and as a couple, that has yet to bloom. These gifts may have been evident years before but just need to be stirred up and repositioned for your spring to arrive.

My Prayer

Thank you, Lord. Even after the coldest of winters, you stir up and reveal the beauty you have planted within us. Help us to realize how each season in our lives is an opportunity to dig deeper and grow stronger. Even when we're weary, keep our eyes and our actions focused on you, faithful, as you are faithful.

Amen.

Devotional Stories for Wives

Meet Our Contributors
Meet Our Authors
Thank You
About Chicken Soup for the Soul

Meet Our Contributors

Debbie Acklin is a frequent contributor to the *Chicken Soup for the Soul* series. She lives in Alabama with her husband, two children, and Duchess the cat. She loves to travel and read. At this time, she is working on her first novel. E-mail her at d_acklin@hotmail.com.

Barbara Alpert resides on the west coast of Florida. She enjoys writing and is a published author. She is working on two additional books with the goal of aiding hurting women. She is an active member of her church and leads a women's small group.

Multi-award-winning author **Diana M. Amadeo** sports a bit of pride in having 500+ publications with her byline in books, anthologies, magazines, newspapers and online. Yet, she humbly, persistently tweaks and rewrites her thousand or so rejections with eternal hope that they may yet see the light of day.

Linda Apple is the author of *Inspire! Writing from the Soul* and *Connect! A Simple Guide to Public Speaking for Writers*. She also writes women's fiction. Linda conducts writing and speaking workshops for conferences and serves as the Arkansas Regional Speaker trainer for Stonecroft Ministries. E-mail her at lindacapple@gmail.com.

Deanna Baird is thankful for the support and love of her husband, David. Her devotions have appeared in *The Upper Room*, *Daily Devotions for Writers* and happily, in the *Chicken Soup for the Soul* series.

This is for all who have encouraged her to be more "transparent." E-mail Deanna at deanna.baird@gmail.com.

Susan Barclay is a librarian and writer. She has published short stories and short nonfiction for adults and is actively seeking a publisher for her children's picture books. Susan lives in Ontario, Canada with her husband, teenaged children, and Jazz. Learn more at susan-barclay.ca.

Alma Barkman is the author of eight Christian books plus numerous freelance articles in a wide variety of periodicals. Retired, she enjoys quilting and photography. Learn more at almabarkman.com.

Sarah Bergman lives in a small Kansas town with her beloved husband and teenage children. She is a Children's Ministry Director and enjoys getting to share God's love with the children of her community. She plans to write more inspirational stories and children's books. E-mail her at zron55@hotmail.com.

Jennie Bradstreet is a freelance writer. She is a wife and mother, and has been a stay-at-home mom for eighteen years. Her family has been through many struggles and adventures, including a premature baby, a house fire, three floods and cancer, all of which have given Jennie a unique perspective on life. E-mail her at bejennie1@gmail.com.

Barbara Brady is a retired RN who lives in Topeka, KS. She enjoys travel and, with her husband Merris, has visited every continent. She's an avid reader and active member of the Kansas Authors Club.

Mary Wood Bridgman is a lawyer and native Floridian. Her work has appeared in national, regional, and local publications. Mary has been a frequent contributor to her hometown newspaper as well as a local NPR affiliate station.

Deanna Broome is a Christian Life Coach, author, and speaker. She received her master's degree in marriage and family therapy at Liberty University in 2012. Her specific calling is working in women's ministry and assisting her husband with marriage workshops and seminars. E-mail her at deannabroome@gmail.com.

Debra Ayers Brown is a writer, humorist, blogger, magazine columnist, and award-winning marketing professional. Her stories have appeared in *Chicken Soup for the Soul* books, *Guideposts*, *Woman's World*, *Liberty Life*, and others. She is a Southeastern Writers Association Board Member. Connect with her at About.Me/DebraAyersBrown.

Diane Buller lives in central Illinois. She taught high school and college writing for more than thirty years and is the published author of other devotions, newspaper articles, and stories, including one in *Chicken Soup for the Soul: New Moms*.

Jeni Bullis is a stay-at-home mom from Sherwood, OR. She has been a partner in worship ministry with her husband Dan for the past eighteen years. Jeni is passionate about women's ministry, parenting and marriage. Her blog, "On My Heart," was where she discovered a love for and interest in writing.

Betsy Burnett is a freelance writer, crafting event planner and children's ministry director. She currently lives in Illinois with her husband and four children whom she homeschools. In her free time, Betsy enjoys riding her bike, reading, and crafts of all types. E-mail her at burnett.betsy@gmail.com.

Dawn Byrne writes full-time about families and relationships, both fictional and nonfictional. She is a member of The South Jersey Writers' Group and two other writing groups. Dawn teaches Sunday school and loves reading. She is currently working on a young adult novel.

Jennifer Cardine spends most of her time with her three young children. She is a licensed counselor with a B.S. degree in behavioral science and an M.A. degree in clinical and counseling psychology. When she has a quiet moment, she enjoys writing. She and her family live in New York.

Amber Cavalier is a Catholic wife and mother who enjoys finding little miracles in everyday life. Amber is also a nurse. She loves to make people laugh and dreams of seeing her name in print, in something other than her obituary. E-mail her at cavalier.amber@yahoo.com.

Kelly Combs, wife, mom, writer, and speaker, has been published in *Guideposts*, *Love Is a Verb* devotional, and many other venues. Visit her website at kellycombs.com, where you'll find a link to her devotional blog, "Chatty Kelly." She loves to hear from her readers at chattykelly@comcast.net.

Eleanor Cowles graduated from University of Illinois and Presbyterian Hospital School of Nursing in Chicago. She worked in nursing, was blessed with three sons, and now enjoys retirement with her husband. Eleanor likes quilting and gardening, and writes for a small monthly Christian newspaper, mostly devotionals and poetry.

Michelle Crystal is the wife of one and the mother of four. She has written three full-length novels that are being considered for publication, and is actively working on her fourth. Michelle enjoys exercise, working with children, and writing. E-mail her at michellecrystal@comcast.net.

Linda C. Defew started writing ten years ago when rheumatoid arthritis hit so hard it led to typing with only one hand. With her faith in God and a strong determination, she began writing about her illness in an effort to inspire others like herself. E-mail her at oldest@tds.net.

Lynn Dove is the author of award-winning contemporary Christian books in *The Wounded Trilogy*. Her blog, "Journey Thoughts," won a Canadian Christian Writing Award in 2011. She has written for *HomeLife* and *Parenting Teens* magazines (LifeWay), as well as *Chicken Soup for the Soul: Parenthood*. Learn more at lynndove.wordpress.com.

Shawnelle Eliasen and her husband Lonny raise their brood of boys in Illinois. Her stories have been published in *Guideposts*, *MomSense* magazine, *Marriage Partnership*, *Thriving Family*, *Cup of Comfort* books, numerous titles in the *Chicken Soup for the Soul* anthology, and more. Visit her blog, "Family Grace with My Five Sons," at Shawnellewrites.blogspot.com.

Susan Farr Fahncke has been published in over seventy books and is the author of *Angel's Legacy: How Cancer Changed a Princess into an Angel*. Her volunteer group, Angels2TheHeart, supports people battling cancer and other serious illnesses. Learn more or take an online writing workshop at 2TheHeart.com.

Andrea Fortenberry lives near Phoenix, AZ with her husband and two children. She writes and speaks on relationships, family issues and faith. She has a journalism degree from Pepperdine University and is a graduate of She Speaks, a program of Proverbs 31 Ministries. Connect with Andrea at andreafortenberry.com.

Tina Friesen has planted a church, lived overseas as a missionary, owned a tearoom, performed in various music bands, and exhibited her watercolor paintings. She completed her Bachelor of Arts degree, with highest honours in counseling, after the birth of her first grandchild. E-mail her at friesentina@gmail.com.

Diane Gardner holds a Bachelor of Arts and a Master of Arts degree in mass communication and journalism from California State University, Fresno. She is a full-time freelance writer and editor. Diane lives in the San Francisco Bay Area, where she enjoys traveling, painting, reading, and attending local community events.

Nancy B. Gibbs is a pastor's wife, and a mother and grandmother. She is the author of ten books. She has contributed numerous stories to the *Chicken Soup for the Soul* series, newspapers and magazines. She speaks at churches, businesses and civic organizations nationwide. Contact her at nancybgibbs.com or nancybgibbs@aol.com.

Phyllis Tomberg Giglio is an inspirational speaker and author. In her autobiography, *When You Come to the End of Your Rope There Is Hope*, she describes her life as the mother of six sons and six daughters. She loves family gatherings. Her hobbies are reading and Bible studies.

Carla J. Giomo is a composer, writer, educator, and sound therapist. She has a B.M. and M.A. degree in music (piano performance) and a Ph.D. in music education. She and her husband, Luciano, enjoy doing many things together, including playing with their two adorable cats. Learn more at MusicAndSpirit.com and SoundHealthAZ.com.

Marge Gower is a retired teacher's aide, who worked with special needs children. She lives in Auburn, NY with her husband Jim and their French bulldog, Bugg. Marge has a devotional published in the *Love Is a Verb* anthology and many newsletters. She writes children's stories and inspirational pieces.

Alice King Greenwood earned her Bachelor of Arts degree in English and Master of Arts degree in counseling. She taught school for twenty-five years. She and her husband are the parents of five children and many grandchildren. Alice is active in community and church activities, and enjoys writing poetry and music.

Kim Harms is a freelance writer and lives in Huxley, IA with her adventure-loving husband and three growing sons. In addition to writing, she runs a clothing ministry for Haitian children at 500dresses.

org. You can learn more about her life and her previously published work at kimharms.net.

Dena Harris is a writer, author, wife, and ultra-endurance runner. Her book, *Who Moved My Mouse? A Self-Help Book for Cats*, has been published in six languages. Her next book, *Does This Collar Make My Butt Look Big?*, will be available in late 2013. Learn more at denaharris. com.

Carol Hartsoe and her husband, Joel, live in Bear Creek, NC. She is blessed that her family lives nearby and enjoys spending time with them. Her hobbies include scrapbooking and gardening. A retired teaching assistant, Carol now spends time writing for children. E-mail her at chartsoe@ec.rr.com.

Carol Hatcher is a boot-wearing, coffee-drinking Christian author, speaker, wife and mother. She believes we can all be everyday missionaries by serving "the least of these." Carol lives in Buford, GA with her husband and three children. Learn more at sheeptotheright. com.

A freelance writer from upstate New York, **Wendy Hobday Haugh's** articles and short stories have appeared in dozens of national magazines, including *Woman's World* and *Highlights for Children*. A mother of three and grandmother of four, she lives with her husband of thirty years and their two spoiled felines. E-mail her at whhaugh@ nycap.rr.com.

Marijo Herndon lives in New York with her husband, Dave, and two cats, Lucy and Ethel. She has written several stories for the *Chicken Soup for the Soul* series, NightsAndWeekends.com, *Not Your Mother's Book* series, *One Touch from the Maker*, *Simple Joy*, and *The Daily Gazette*.

Julie Hornok has been married to her wonderful husband for sixteen years and is the mother of three children, including a daughter with autism. Julie enjoys writing about the constant (and sometimes painfully real) ups and downs of her family's journey through life with autism. E-mail her at julie_hornok@yahoo.com.

Marcia Hornok, managing editor of *CHERA Fellowship* magazine for widowed people, lives in Utah where her husband pastors Midvalley Bible Church. Their six children have rewarded them with nine grandkids so far. Marcia writes for numerous periodicals, examiner. com, and devotional books including *Fruit of the Spirit: Inspiration for Women*.

Teresa Hoy lives in rural Missouri with her husband and a large family of rescued cats and dogs. Her work has appeared in a number of publications, including the *Chicken Soup for the Soul* series, *The Ultimate* books, *Rural Missouri* magazine, and *The Mid-America Poetry Review*. Learn more at teresahoy.com.

When not spending time with her husband and son, **Jeanette Hurt** writes books, articles and essays, primarily about food, wine and travel. She also teaches culinary and writing classes. Follow her on Twitter, @JHurtAuthor, or visit her website at jeanettehurt.com.

Pamela Jarmon-Wade, M.B.A., is the author of *The Adventures of Little Leroy: The Legacy of Martin Luther King, Jr.* She has appeared in several independent films and the stage play, *When Children Pray*. She enjoys her church, family, and traveling. Learn more at pamelajarmonwade. com.

Katie Cromwell Johnson is married to a cattle rancher, the mother of two boys, and a middle school counselor. She spends her spare time reading, writing, singing, riding horses, helping on the farm, woods rambling, traveling, and spending time with friends and family. E-mail her at kjohnson0797@gmail.com.

Pat Stockett Johnston was a missionary in Lebanon, Jordan, and Papua New Guinea for thirty-four years. She oversaw the printing of religious material in Arabic, Armenian, and Melanesian Pidgin. Pat enjoys writing, teaching, speaking, and growing mums and roses for show. E-mail her at writerpat@att.net.

Vicki Julian is the author of three inspirational books, as well as a contributor of articles and stories to various magazines, newspapers and anthologies. She is a Stephen Minister, citizen journalist for *The Humanitarian Examiner*, and a Board Member of the Kansas Authors Club. Contact her at vickijulian.com.

Writing and worshiping are **Sandy Knudsen's** primary passions. She is working on her first book. It will tell the story of how her disabled husband lived a life of passion and purpose in spite of his infirmity. She enjoys spending time with her family and friends. E-mail her at worshipatrest@gmail.com.

Becky Kopitzke is a freelance writer, devotional blogger and family cheerleader. She and her husband enjoy pushing swings and pulling sleds for their two lovely daughters in Northeast Wisconsin. They now schedule monthly date nights without fail. Read more at beckykopitzke.blogspot.com.

Joanne Kraft is a mom of four and the author of *Just Too Busy: Taking Your Family on a Radical Sabbatical*. She and her husband Paul recently moved their family from California to Tennessee, and happily traded soymilk and arugula for sweet tea and biscuits. Visit her at JoanneKraft.com.

Cathi LaMarche is a novelist, essayist, educator, and college essay writing coach. Her work appears in numerous anthologies. Residing in Missouri with her husband, two children, and three dogs, she enjoys reading, cooking, and gardening—simple pleasures to balance out the hectic pace of everyday life.

"Nutty with a dash of meat" best describes **Jeanette Levellie's** speaking, writing, and life. She's published hundreds of columns, articles, poems, and a book, *Two Scoops of Grace with Chuckles on Top*. Jeanette is the wife of one, mother of two, grandmother of three, and waitress to four cats. Learn more at jeanettelevellie.com.

Janeen Lewis lives in Georgia with her husband, Jesse, and two children, Andrew and Gracie. Her stories about motherhood and family life have been published in several *Chicken Soup for the Soul* anthologies. E-mail her at jlewis0402@netzero.net.

Dawn M. Lilly lives with her husband in the beautiful Pacific Northwest where she writes, gardens, and loves spending time with her children and grandchildren. This is her fourth story published in the *Chicken Soup for the Soul* series. She is currently working on a novel and welcomes you to learn more at dawnmlilly.com.

Lisa Littlewood is a freelance writer and full-time mom who lives near Buffalo, NY, with her three energetic girls and a very outnumbered (and lucky!) husband. She enjoys writing inspirational and candid stories about her life as a mom and wife. Read more on her blog at www.littlewritermomma.com.

Brenda Louque received her nursing degree from Danville School of Practical Nursing in 1984. She participates in many bereaved parent support groups. She has been published in grief support magazines as well as the *Chicken Soup for the Soul* series.

The marriage described in her story is the second marriage for **DV Mason**, thus the commitment to keep it happy. DV enjoys writing nonfiction short pieces. She divides her time between being a wife, grandmother, and skills trainer for their adult son who has disabilities, and caring for her ninety-five-year-old mother.

Linda Kosinski Maynard is a grandmother from Glastonbury, CT.

Besides writing, she is a floral designer, calligrapher, artist, and even a "sometimes" clown. She volunteers at nursing homes, as well as mentors at-risk children. Her greatest delight is encouraging others. E-mail her at somethingbeautiful.linmaynard@aol.com.

Dayna E. Mazzuca is a long-time writer, instructor and poet. She earned her degree in Political Philosophy in 1990 and diploma in Journalism Arts four years later. Her work appears online, and in newspapers and magazines. When not beachcombing, she homeschools her two children on Vancouver Island. Learn more at daynawrites.blogspot.com.

Linda Mehus-Barber is a teacher and freelance writer who lives with her husband and two dogs in Langley, B.C. Their little cabin overflows with the love and joy that comes from seeking life's simple pleasures.

Michelle Close Mills' poetry and short stories have appeared in many magazines and anthologies, including several *Chicken Soup for the Soul* books. Michelle resides in west central Florida, is married and is Mom to two kids, three cockatiels and two precious rescue kitties. Learn more at authorsden.com/michelleclosemills.

Sherrie Murphree, of Odessa, TX, is a freelance writer of inspirational articles, devotionals, and puzzles she uses in the Bible class she teaches. Published in thirty different magazines and ten book compilations, she loves to encourage others in their writing. She serves as a church musician. Her daughter is Valerie.

Krisan Murphy, a wife of thirty-two years and mother of four, considers herself a cheerleader of those who seek Jesus and a guide to those who don't. With a B.A. degree in English, she works as a writer, homeschooling mom, and doorman for the family pets.

Dena Netherton is a classically trained singer, pianist, and guitarist.

Her stories and articles appear in several Christian publications. Dena and her husband live in the beautiful Colorado Rocky Mountains. Check out her blog at denanetherton.blogspot.com.

Janice Flood Nichols holds a B.A. degree from Seton Hill College and a M.Ed. degree from the University of Pittsburgh. She is the author of *Twin Voices: A Memoir of Polio, the Forgotten Killer*. She devotes her time to polio eradication efforts. This is her sixth story published in the *Chicken Soup for the Soul* series.

Tammy Nischan is a Christian teacher, writer, and speaker. As the mother of six, two of whom are in heaven, Tammy's passion is ministering to other grieving moms. She would love to hear from you! Visit her on her blog, "My Heart His Words" at tammynischan. blogspot.com, or follow her on Twitter @ilovepennies.

Married since 2006, **Joan Oen** and her husband Shawn live in Minnesota with their young son. Joan teaches English and has a Master of Arts degree in Human Development. To learn about Joan and her stepdaughter, read "That's What Moms Are For" in *Chicken Soup for the Soul: The Magic of Mothers and Daughters*.

Andrea Arthur Owan is a writer, speaker, educator, and health and fitness professional. She lives in Arizona with her beloved, Chris, and their younger child. Her blog, brokenheartsredeemed.blogspot. com, helps families heal emotionally, physically and spiritually from the loss of a child during pregnancy or at birth. E-mail her at andreaarthurowan@gmail.com.

Nancy Peacock is a writer of novels and short stories. She loves to garden and read. Her husband and three daughters support her writing.

Holli Pearson, author of *Straight from the Heart, Prayers for Everyday Living* (2008), has been a Bible study leader for twenty-one years. She is currently "Thursday Live" Director for Women's Bible studies at Church of the Resurrection in Leawood, KS. E-mail her at holliouya@gmail.com.

Mary C. M. Phillips is a caffeinated wife, mother, and writer. She blogs at CaffeinatedWord.wordpress.com. Follow her on Twitter @ marycmphil.

Stephanie Piro lives in New Hampshire with her husband and three cats. She is one of King Features' "Six Chix" (she is the Saturday chick!). Her single panel, "Fair Game," appears in newspapers and on her website: www.stephaniepiro.com. She is also an illustrator, a designer of gift items for her company Strip T's, and a part-time librarian. Contact her at stephaniepiro@gmail.com.

Kay Conner Pliszka has been published in seventeen *Chicken Soup for the Soul* books. She is a motivational speaker, using her stories to help others. Through her humor and honesty, Kay is able to comfort and inspire her readers and audiences. E-mail her at kmpliszka@comcast.net.

Kimberly Porrazzo is editor-in-chief at Freedom Communications and the *Orange County Register*, where she oversees three magazines and websites, including *Orange County Register Family* magazine. Married to her college sweetheart for thirty-two years, they have two adult sons together. She is working on her first novel. Learn more at Kimberlyporrazzo.com.

Amelia Rhodes is the author of *Isn't It Time for a Coffee Break? Doing Life Together in an All-About-Me Kind of World*. She lives in Michigan with her husband and children. When the Michigan weather cooperates, she enjoys running and gardening with her family. E-mail her at amelia@ameliarhodes.com.

Many of **Ann Robertson's** writings and paintings originate from her captivation and curiosity in nature. Her expressions have a hidden agenda, though: to encourage healing and peace to those broken by a painful past. Ann's love for God and her lessons in life are shared bi-monthly at annelizabethrobertson.com.

Jeneil Palmer Russell blogs at rhemashope.wordpress.com about life with her Army husband Brandon and their daughters: Rhema, who is nine, autistic, epileptic, beautiful, brilliant, funny and gentle-hearted; and Hope, who is six, silly, joyful, imaginative, kind and full of all the best of childhood. Jeneil is author of *Sunburned Faces.*

Amy Sayers is a fifth-grade teacher, mother, childbirth educator, captain on the sideline at Notre Dame Stadium, and most importantly, the wife of David. As a survivor of epilepsy, she uses her story to encourage others to find their JOY during difficult times.

Sara Schafer is a two-time cancer survivor who is married with two children and a grandson. She cross-stitches Christian bookmarks, and writes nonfiction inspirational stories and daily devotionals. Her story, "Hope in the ICU," was published in *Chicken Soup for the Soul: Angels Among Us.* E-mail her at sara757s@aol.com.

Bev Schwind has published anthologies and devotions, and written five books. She was Patches on the television show *Patches and Pockets* for eighteen years. A retired nurse, Bev teaches weekly at a jail and rehab center. She and her husband of sixty years, Jim, have won tennis medals in Senior Olympics. E-mail her at Bevschwind@hotmail.com.

Michelle Shocklee is a writer who desires to give God glory with each word, whether through inspirational fiction, true-life stories, or blog posts that are read by people all around the globe. Her greatest pleasure is spending time with her family. Learn more at michelleshocklee.com.

Tracey L. Simpson, a freelance writer, finds inspiration sitting beside her lake, relaxing and observing wildlife in rural Missouri. She enjoys writing, antiquing and spending time with her children, Ashley and Austin, her husband and their menagerie of pets.

Diane Stark is a wife and mother of five. She loves to write about the important things in life: her family and her faith. She is a frequent contributor to the *Chicken Soup for the Soul* series, as well as dozens of magazines. E-mail her at DianeStark19@yahoo.com.

Johnna Stein has been happily married to her Dutchman for twenty-three years. With two kids in college, she began a new career as a foster care advocate. Johnna's learning to write "in between" and hopes her YA novel in verse, *he said he loved me*, will find a publisher soon.

Amy L. Stout is a wife, mommy, and autism advocate who loves travel, coffeehouses, books and, most importantly, Jesus! As a child of the King, her tiara is often missing, dusty, bent out of shape or crooked, but she will always and forever be his treasured princess. Learn more at histreasuredprincess.blogspot.com.

Deborah Sturgill is a Christian Life Coach with a focus on God's amazing grace. She works with women who want to discover "Who I am in Christ," develop a self-care plan, and live a life of purpose. Visit her website/blog at christianwomencoach.com or e-mail her at debbie@christianwomencoach.com.

Donna Teti loves to write inspirational stories and poems that will lift a person's spirit. She has previously been published in the *Chicken Soup for the Soul* series, *Guideposts*, and many compilation books. Enjoy more of Donna's inspirational stories and poems at donnateti.com or facebook.com/TwinpopInspirations.

Jayne Thurber-Smith is an award-winning writer for various publications, including *Faith & Friends*, *Floral Business* magazine and *The Buffalo News*, and is a sports contributor to CBN.com. Her and her husband's favorite activity is being included in whatever their four adult children have going on. E-mail her at jthurbersmith@cox.net.

Author of more than one hundred articles, **Sue Tornai** lives with her husband, John, and dog, Maggie, in Northern California. Her most rewarding experience in writing is when someone tells her one of her stories touched a heart or changed a life.

Marilyn Turk received her degree in journalism and wrote advertising copy before pursuing a sales career. After retirement, she began writing again, and has been published in magazines and the *Chicken Soup for the Soul* series. She and her husband live in Florida and enjoy researching lighthouses and Southern Civil War history. Learn more at pathwayheart.com and read her lighthouse blog.

Brittany Valentine, a Clemson University graduate, resides in Simpsonville, SC. She wears many hats, including wife, mother of three boys, homeschool teacher and writer. Her passion is Bible literacy and application. She is available to speak at women's events on a variety of topics. E-mail her at mbval323@yahoo.com.

Pamela Louise Walker is a mother, wife and observer of life. She and her husband share their Midwestern farm with their three homeschooled littles, her octogenarian mother, and a menagerie of chickens, cats and dogs. Take a peek inside her "never a dull moment" life at thespottedhen.blogspot.com.

Emily Weaver is a freelance writer living in Springfield, MO with her husband and three children. She enjoys traveling, spending time with her family, and chronicling the crazy and off-the-wall experiences of motherhood in her blog, www.abettermomthanme.blogspot.com. E-mail her at emily-weaver@sbcglobal.net.

Sarah Wessels and her husband Matt raise their family on a quiet parcel of land in rural Illinois. They own/operate a family business and home-teach their four children. Sarah enjoys painting, reading, writing, and watching and playing sports. Read her blog, "Daily Chaotic Bliss," at dailychaoticbliss.blogspot.com.

Angela Wolthuis lives in the woods of Alberta with her husband and three boys. She finds inspiration for her writing in everything around her, and loves to quilt, craft and be active. Last year she published her first book. E-mail Angela at angwolthuis@me.com.

Sheri Zeck enjoys writing creative nonfiction stories that encourage, inspire and entertain others. She lives in Milan, IL with her husband and three daughters. She has contributed stories to the *Chicken Soup for the Soul* series, *Guideposts*, *Farm & Ranch Living* and various other magazines. Visit her website at sherizeck.com.

Meet Our Authors

Susan M. Heim is a longstanding author and editor, specializing in parenting, women's and Christian issues. After the birth of her twin boys in 2003, Susan left her desk job as a Senior Editor at a publishing company and has never looked back. Being a work-at-home mother allows her to follow her two greatest passions: parenting and writing.

Susan's published books include the *Chicken Soup for the Soul: Devotional Stories* series; *Chicken Soup for the Soul: Inspiration for Writers*; *Chicken Soup for the Soul: Finding My Faith*; *Chicken Soup for the Soul: Here Comes the Bride*; *Chicken Soup for the Soul: New Moms*; *Chicken Soup for the Soul: Family Matters*; *Chicken Soup for the Soul: All in the Family*; *Chicken Soup for the Soul: Twins and More*; *Boosting Your Baby's Brain Power*; *It's Twins! Parent-to-Parent Advice from Infancy Through Adolescence*; *Oh, Baby! 7 Ways a Baby Will Change Your Life the First Year*; and *Twice the Love: Stories of Inspiration for Families with Twins, Multiples and Singletons*.

Susan's articles and stories have appeared in many books, websites, and magazines, including *TWINS Magazine* and *Angels on Earth*. Her blogs include: Susan Heim on Parenting at susanheim.blogspot.com and Susan Heim on Writing at www.susanheimonwriting.com. She is the founder of TwinsTalk, a website with tips, advice and stories about raising twins and multiples, at www.twinstalk.com.

Susan and her husband Mike are the parents of four sons, who are in elementary school and college! You can reach Susan at susan@susanheim.com and visit her website at www.susanheim.

com. Join her on Twitter, Facebook and Pinterest by searching for ParentingAuthor.

Karen C. Talcott is the co-author of the devotional books published by Chicken Soup for the Soul, including *Chicken Soup for the Soul: Devotional Stories for Women*, *Chicken Soup for the Soul: Devotional Stories for Mothers* and *Chicken Soup for the Soul: Devotional Stories for Tough Times*. Her work was also included in *Chicken Soup for the Soul: Twins and More* and most recently in *Chicken Soup for the Soul: Parenthood*. She has a variety of new projects in the works, including several children's books and many more devotional short stories.

Karen's experience in writing came from fifteen years in the classroom and a master's degree in curriculum from Oregon State University. While no longer teaching elementary school, Karen continues to share her experiences and knowledge through her writing and speaking engagements. After the birth of her twins and caring for a two-and-a-half-year-old daughter, Karen decided to focus her attention on freelance writing. Her husband, Leland, and three children, Kara, Griffin, and Taylor, are very supportive of her writing, and for this she is thankful.

Born in the beautiful state of Oregon, Karen now resides in Florida. She finds her best inspiration comes in the morning on her long walks with her two Golden Retrievers. Story ideas and titles seem to flow as she communes in God's world. Working on the *Chicken Soup for the Soul* devotional series has been one of her most rewarding writing endeavors. Reading the stories, scriptures, and prayers by the many contributors has affected her life in a very personal way. She is thankful to be a part of this amazing series and knows that God's mighty hand is in each and every one of the stories collected. It is her hope that you, the reader, will also find God's amazing grace in the pages of this book.

In her spare time, what precious moments there are, she enjoys her children and their many sports and activities, gardening, walking, and faithfully attending her local church. She can be reached at Kartalcott@aol.com.

Thank You

*W*e appreciate all of our wonderful family members and friends, who continue to inspire and teach us on our life's journey. We have been blessed beyond measure with their constant love and support.

We owe huge thanks to all of our contributors. We know that you pour your hearts and souls into the stories that you share with us, and ultimately with each other. We appreciate your willingness to open up your lives to other Chicken Soup for the Soul readers. We can only publish a small percentage of the stories that are submitted, but we read every single one, and even those that do not appear in the book have an influence on us and on the final manuscript. We strongly encourage you to continue submitting to future *Chicken Soup for the Soul* books.

We would like to thank Amy Newmark, our Publisher, for her generous spirit, creative vision, and expert editing. We're also grateful to D'ette Corona, our VP and Assistant Publisher, who seamlessly manages a dozen projects at a time while keeping all of us focused and on schedule; Barbara LoMonaco, Chicken Soup for the Soul's Webmaster and Editor, who is always so patient and helpful; and Chicken Soup for the Soul Editor Kristiana Glavin Pastir, for her assistance with the final manuscript and proofreading.

We owe a very special thanks to Stephanie Piro, whose skill in creating just the right cartoons for these devotional stories ensures that we continue to look at the lighter side of life. And to our Creative Director and book producer, Brian Taylor at Pneuma Books, for his brilliant vision for our covers and interiors. Finally, we praise God for guiding us through every step of putting this book together. His presence is truly felt in every page.

Improving Your Life Every Day

Real people sharing real stories—for twenty years. Now, Chicken Soup for the Soul has gone beyond the bookstore to become a world leader in life improvement. Through books, movies, DVDs, online resources and other partnerships, we bring hope, courage, inspiration and love to hundreds of millions of people around the world. Chicken Soup for the Soul's writers and readers belong to a one-of-a-kind global community, sharing advice, support, guidance, comfort, and knowledge.

Chicken Soup for the Soul stories have been translated into more than 40 languages and can be found in more than one hundred countries. Every day, millions of people experience a Chicken Soup for the Soul story in a book, magazine, newspaper or online. As we share our life experiences through these stories, we offer hope, comfort and inspiration to one another. The stories travel from person to person, and from country to country, helping to improve lives everywhere.

Share with Us

We all have had Chicken Soup for the Soul moments in our lives. If you would like to share your story or poem with millions of people around the world, go to chickensoup.com and click on "Submit Your Story." You may be able to help another reader, and become a published author at the same time. Some of our past contributors have launched writing and speaking careers from the publication of their stories in our books!

Our submission volume has been increasing steadily—the quality and quantity of your submissions has been fabulous. We only accept story submissions via our website. They are no longer accepted via mail or fax.

To contact us regarding other matters, please send us an e-mail through webmaster@chickensoupforthesoul.com, or fax or write us at:

Chicken Soup for the Soul
P.O. Box 700
Cos Cob, CT 06807-0700
Fax: 203-861-7194

One more note from your friends at Chicken Soup for the Soul: Occasionally, we receive an unsolicited book manuscript from one of our readers, and we would like to respectfully inform you that we do not accept unsolicited manuscripts and we must discard the ones that appear.

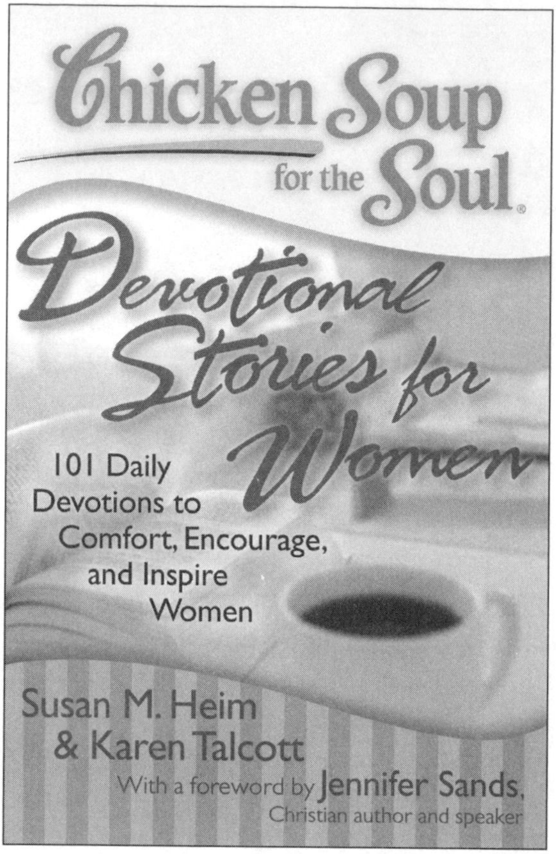

Chicken Soup for the Soul.
for the Soul.

Devotional Stories for Women

101 Daily Devotions to Comfort, Encourage, and Inspire Women

Susan M. Heim & Karen Talcott

With a foreword by Jennifer Sands, Christian author and speaker

Throughout time, women have shared their joys and sorrows, thoughts and feelings, experiences and life lessons with one another. The tradition continues in this charming book with 101 stories of friendship, faith, and comfort that affirm God's unconditional love and His wisdom. Women will find encouragement, solace, and strength in these personal stories and prayers that cover everyday trials, tests of faith, marriage, parenting, service to others, and self-esteem.

978-1-935096-48-1

More devotions

Chicken Soup for the Soul
for the Soul

Devotional Stories for Mothers

101 Daily Devotions to Comfort, Encourage, and Inspire Mothers

Susan M. Heim
and Karen C. Talcott
Foreword by Lisa Whelchel

Through the ages, mothers have shared their experiences, thoughts, and feelings with one another. The tradition continues in this book of 101 personal stories and prayers by moms about all aspects of motherhood. This book will uplift, counsel, and reassure any woman of faith who needs a boost or reminder of God's ever-present love as she goes through the ups and downs of life and motherhood.

978-1-935096-53-5

to inspire you!

Struggles test us all, but readers will find counsel and reassurance in these devotional stories of faith, strength, and prayer. This collection is filled with stories that show God's presence during times of trouble — from illness, addictions, job loss, grief, and much more — providing a boost and reminder of God's ever-present love. Readers will find encouragement, solace, and hope in these personal stories and prayers.

978-1-935096-74-0

More hope

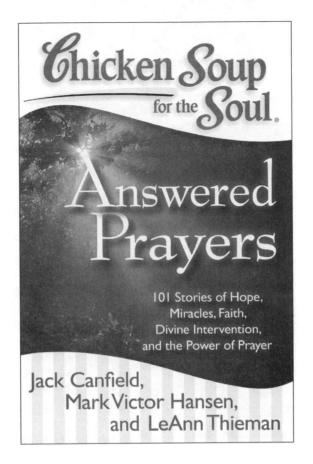

Chicken Soup for the Soul.
for the Soul.

Answered Prayers

101 Stories of Hope,
Miracles, Faith,
Divine Intervention,
and the Power of Prayer

Jack Canfield,
Mark Victor Hansen,
and LeAnn Thieman

We all need help from time to time, and these 101 true stories of answered prayers show a higher power at work in our lives. Regular people share their personal, touching stories of God's Divine intervention, healing power, and communication. Filled with stories about the power of prayer, miracles, and hope, this book will inspire anyone looking to boost his or her faith and read some amazing stories.

978-1-935096-76-4

and inspiration!

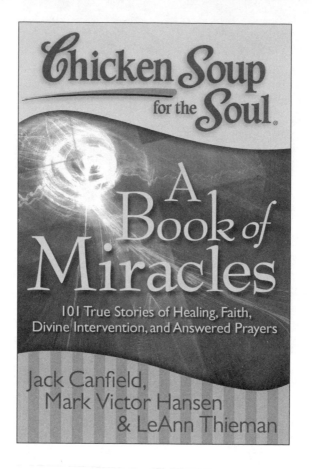

Chicken Soup
for the Soul.

A
Book of
Miracles

101 True Stories of Healing, Faith,
Divine Intervention, and Answered Prayers

Jack Canfield,
Mark Victor Hansen
& LeAnn Thieman

Everyone loves a good miracle story, and this book provides 101 true stories
of healing, divine intervention, and answered prayers. These amazing, personal
stories prove that God is alive and active in the world today, working miracles on
our behalf. The incredible accounts show His love and involvement in our lives.
This book of miracles will encourage, uplift, and recharge the faith of Catholics
and all Christian readers.

978-1-935096-51-1

Miracles

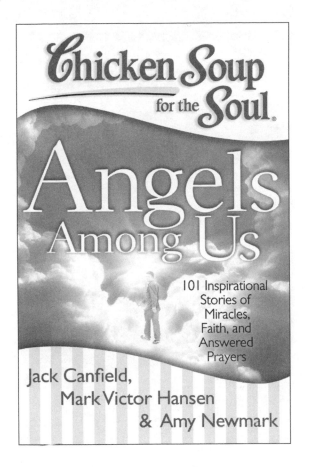

Celestial, otherworldly, heavenly. Whatever the term, sometimes there is no earthly explanation for what we experience, and a higher power is clearly at work. In this book of 101 inspirational stories, contributors share their personal angel experiences of faith, miracles, and answered prayers. You will be awed and inspired by these true personal stories from people, religious and non-religious, about angel guidance, miraculous intervention, and love from beyond.

978-1-61159-906-0

can happen!

Chicken Soup for the Soul

for the Soul

Messages from Heaven

The National Bestseller with Real Stories from Real People

101 **Miraculous** Stories of **Signs** from Beyond, Amazing **Connections**, and **Love** that Doesn't Die

Jack Canfield,
Mark Victor Hansen,
and Amy Newmark

When our loved ones leave this world, our connection with them does not end. Sometimes when we see or hear from them, they give us signs and messages. Sometimes they speak to us in dreams or they appear in different forms. The stories in this book, both religious and secular, will amaze you, giving you new knowledge, insight and awareness about the connection and communication we have with those who have passed on or those who have experienced dying and coming back.

978-1-935096-91-7

More love